Gifts from God

Gifts from God

encouragement and hope
for today's parents

Dr. David Jeremiah

Chariot Victor Publishing
A Division of Cook Communications

Chariot Victor Publishing
Cook Communications, Colorado Springs, Colorado 80918
Cook Communications, Paris, Ontario, Canada
Kingsway Communications, Eastbourne, England

Unless otherwise indicated, Scripture quotations are from *The New King James Version,* © 1979, 1980, 1982, Thomas Nelson, Inc., Publishers. Other quotations are from the *New American Standard Bible* (NASB), the Lockman Foundation © 1960, 1962, 1963, 1968, 1971, 1972, 1973, 1975, 1977; the *Holy Bible: New International Version*® (NIV). Copyright © 1973, 1978, 1984 by International Bible Society. Used by permission of Zondervan Publishing House. All rights reserved; and *The Living Bible* (TLB), © 1971, Tyndale House Publishers, Wheaton, IL 60189. Used by permission.

An effort has been made to locate sources and obtain permission, where necessary, for the quotations used in this book. In the event of an unintentional omission, a modification will gladly be incorporated in future printings.

Cover and Interior Design: Image Studios
Cover Photography: Photodisc

1 2 3 4 5 6 7 8 9 10 Printing / Year 03 02 01 00 99

Published in association with Sealy M. Yates, Literary Agent, Orange, California.

Library of Congress Cataloging–in–Publication Data

Jeremiah, David.
    Gifts from God : encouraging words for parents/David Jeremiah.
       p. cm.
    Includes bibliographical references.
    ISBN 1-56476-766-3
    1. Parents--Religious life.   2. Parenting--Religious aspects--Christianity.   I. Title.
      BV4529.J47   1999
      248.8'45--dc21   98-53687
                                                     CIP

Contents

To Donna,
my loving wife,
"the heart and soul of our family."

Acknowledgments

What does it mean to acknowledge someone? My mind pictures a crowded room and as I pass through that room, I passively "acknowledge" someone with a gesture or nod. When you read the word "acknowledgments" at the beginning of a book, do you normally rush past the page because you haven't time for people you don't know? If you're like most of us, you see *acknowledging* someone as just one level above *disregarding* them.

So maybe we should change the title of this page to "Some Profound Thank-You's." It better suits what I want to do here!

First of all, a profound thank-You to my Heavenly Father, who one day said, "It is not good for man to be alone." It was He who started this whole family business! Father God, I love You for allowing me to be a part of Your family and for giving me such a wonderful family here on earth.

John and Jan Dodge, David and Cami Jeremiah, Jennifer Jeremiah, and Daniel Jeremiah, thank you . . . for all you have taught me about love and forgiveness and laughter and commitment and all of the other building blocks of great families. And Donna, I devoted a whole page to give thanks to you, but there are not enough pages in the world to tell the story of my love for you and my deep gratitude for what you mean to all of us. This is our story from beginning to end . . . the story of God's working in the David and Donna Jeremiah family.

Another profound thank-you goes to Helen Barnhart and Glenda Parker. Helen worked with the editors and publishers to see that everything was as they wanted it to be. Glenda administrates my office at Shadow Mountain Community Church and greatly helps to organize my life so that I have time to study and write. What my son David

Michael does to manage things for us at Turning Point is another reason I am able to do what I do!

This project is the very first one to be produced by the editing tandem of Steve Halliday and Larry Libby. I have had the privilege of working with each of these men individually on other projects, but I never dreamed that they would someday join their unique skills in a new partnership called *Crown Media*. I love each of you deeply. You are godly men and are extremely good at what you do. You care about the message and the messenger! I hope we can work together many more times as the Lord directs. A Double Profound Thank-You to you both!

Sealy Yates has been my attorney, literary agent, and personal friend for many years. What he continues to do for me personally and professionally is one of the bright spots in my life. He and his wife Susan continue to model for us the commitment to godly excellence that challenges every member of our family to excel. Tom Thompson, of the Yates & Yates group, has also been a faithful contributor both to the organization and to the preparation of this book.

Finally, I want to say a word of gratitude to Greg Clouse and Chariot Victor Publishing. Greg, along with David Bolthouse of Direct Media, convinced me that this book needed to be written. More and more I am seeing people from different organizations working together for the glory and honor of the Lord. May this spirit of oneness and cooperation continue 'til He comes!

David Jeremiah
December, 1998

Introduction

I'm Still a Learner

I always get a little nervous whenever I'm asked to express my thoughts on successful family living.

At all costs, I want to avoid the impression that I have "arrived"…that I can now speak with full authority on the subject because I do everything right. I may be the father of four grown children and the grandfather of one, but I can assure you that I *don't* do everything right! I'm still a learner, along with everyone else.

Still, God has taught me a great deal through the years, and I long to put my hand on the shoulder of anxious parents (and parents-to-be), encouraging them that, with God's help, they can build solid and loving Christian homes fragrant with the aroma of Christ.

All of us parents need encouragement like that.

We need to hear that despite frightening headlines, cultural pressures, and moral free-fall in our land, our God sits firmly on His heavenly throne and promises to give us the strength and wisdom to build Christian households filled with godliness and laughter.

Although *Gifts from God* contains instruction from God's Word on building healthy families, it is not primarily a book of "instruction." I'd call it a book of *encouragement*. More than anything else, I want to encourage parents that they really can rear sons and daughters who love God and bless their communities. I want to bring assurance to those who have just started out on the road of parenting, and hope to those who may be feeling a little wearied or intimidated by the journey. I want to declare to both groups that "with God, all things are possible"–even the seemingly impossible task of building thriving Christian families.

Listen, friend, our sovereign God isn't surprised by any cultural trend in today's world. He isn't shocked by the evening news. He isn't stunned by the condition of public schools. He isn't surprised or shaken by the content of network television. He knew about this era of our history before it ever arrived on our calendars. He knew what would happen–everything–before the foundation of the earth. He knows very well "what kind of world" young children must grow up in today.

And He is as able today as He was yesterday or fifty years ago or a thousand years ago to supply His people with power and wisdom and insight and blessing. Even as we enter this new millennium, moms and dads who draw their strength from Jesus Christ are as able to raise solid, godly families as Christian parents in the 1950s. God doesn't change! His grace is ever available!

If you doubt that, just chew on these words of Paul for a minute or two:

> And God is able to make all grace abound to you, so that
> in all things at all times, having all that you need, you will
> abound in every good work (2 Corinthians 9:8, NIV).

All grace. In all things. At all times. With all that you need. So that you will abound or excel in every good work...*including child-rearing.*

Throughout this book you will hear me loudly cheering you on and shouting, "You can do it!" I do so because I really believe you can do it. Why do I believe this so strongly? Because God never gives us a task without also giving us the resources to successfully complete that task. When He tells us to "train a child in the way he should go" (Proverbs 22:6), He also promises that "if any of you lacks wisdom, let him ask of God, who gives to all liberally and without reproach, and it will be given to him" (James 1:5).

Yes, we moms and dads have a challenging job. But not a hopeless one! Not as long as we depend on the God who tells us, "Be strong and take heart, all you who hope in the LORD" (Psalm 31:24, NIV).

And anyway, who says that parenting and raising a healthy family has to be a burdensome, fearful enterprise that almost inevitably ends in tears? Who made up that fiction, anyway? Even secular psychologists are beginning to see the foolishness of such doomsaying:

A few months ago I was in a major metropolitan mall and wandered into one of the bookstores. Arriving at the child care section, I found myself looking at a row of bookshelves 6 feet tall and 15 feet long: 90 square feet of titles, covering every conceivable aspect of the child and its proper upbringing. There were books on only children, middle children, gifted children, strong-willed children, shy children, learning-disabled children, children with attention deficit disorder, adopted children, and children who don't act like children. There were books on how to toilet train 'em, put 'em to bed, boost their IQs, help with homework, end sibling rivalry, cultivate copious amounts of self esteem, and…you get the picture, I'm sure.

I suddenly realized we child-rearing "experts" have led parents to believe that, in order to properly raise the late-20th century child, you must first consult a psychologist to find out what kind of child you have. From there, you go straight to the bookstore and buy every book you can on that particular permutation of childhood, thus assuring at least a modicum of success. We've also thoroughly mystified what was once thought to be a fairly simple endeavor. Not even Dr. Spock, I'm sure, could have anticipated the torrent of professional posturing on "parenting" that his little child-rearing cookbook unleashed. And what a torrent of babble it has been![1]

The author of this reassuring piece, family psychologist John K. Rosemond, then admitted, "I confess that I have contributed five books and over 1,000 weekly newspaper columns and magazine articles to this torrent. I didn't know what I was doing. I was only trying to meet my deadlines. My editors made me do it. What can I say?"[2]

Bottom line? Rosemond declared himself "guilty–guilty of contributing to the entirely false notion that raising a child is complex, difficult, demanding, draining, exasperating, and so on. Granted, some children

are more difficult than others, and with every child there will be difficult moments, but raising children is not, in general, what people like
myself have made it out to be. Please accept my apologies."³

When was the last time you heard an admission like *that*?

But we musn't stop there. Of all parents, Christian moms and dads
can enjoy the greatest hope, the most confidence, the best encouragement, and the most penetrating insights because they don't have to
tackle this great child-rearing adventure by themselves. In difficult times
they can lean on much more than the wisdom of Dr. Spock; they
possess an open invitation to climb on the shoulders of almighty God
Himself! As Psalm 115:14-15 says,

> May the LORD give you increase more and more,
> You and your children.
> May you be blessed by the LORD,
> Who made heaven and earth.

And don't think this divine resource is only short-term or once-in-
a while! Psalm 103:17 assures us that

> The mercy of the LORD is from everlasting to everlasting
> On those who fear Him,
> And His righteousness to children's children.

Nor does God bestow His blessings sparingly or begrudgingly, as
He Himself declares, "Oh, that they had such a heart in them that they
would fear Me and always keep all My commandments, that it might
be well with them and with their children forever!" (Deuteronomy 5:29)

Now, *that's* encouragement!

Parents, you have every reason to take heart.

Christian mom and dad, you have resources greater than you imagine.

God promises that this adventure of a lifetime comes with heavenly
resources to match. *You can do it!* You can rear delightful sons and
daughters who fear the Lord (and who bless their parents). You can
build a warm, loving home and leave a rich heritage for your children
and your children's children, a legacy that pours untold blessing into

generations yet unborn.

I don't know all there is to know about parenting and rearing kids, but I know one thing at least: God the Father does know everything about how to create families that honor Jesus Christ, and He offers to partner with you in the construction of your home. You could refuse the offer, but why? In my almost thirty years of parenting, I have learned that God is a peerless home builder. I encourage you to make Him your foreman (then watch your house take shape, room by magnificent room).

You really can do it!

---

1 John K. Rosemond, "10 Big Deals That Aren't," *Hemispheres*, June 1994, 104.

2 Ibid.

3 Ibid., 107.

One

The High Privilege & Great Challenge of Parenting

"No culture has ever been able to provide

a better shipyard for building storm-proof vessels

for the journey of man from the cradle

to the grave than the individual nourished

in a loving family."

—LAURENS VAN DER POST AND JANE TAYLOR

Back in the days when women did a lot of home perms, a mother was getting ready for a late date with her husband. While rinsing her hair in the kitchen sink, she heard the unmistakable rustlings of two little boys who were supposed to be in bed.

Lifting her mouth above the stream of hot tap water, she hollered, "You kids get back in bed!" The little boy noises quickly subsided, but as soon as she lathered up again, once more the telltale thumps and bangings wafted down from upstairs. Now beginning to get angry, the mother wrapped a towel around her head, marched over to the foot of the stairs, and yelled, "The next time I hear you, I'm coming up there!"

Confident her threat would eliminate the problem, she returned to the sink to finish her hair. But no sooner were her trusses underwater once more than she heard her kids running around. Furious, she again threw the towel around her head, bounded upstairs, stormed into the room where her two boys were playing and scolded loudly, "I told you to get in bed, I mean for you to get in bed, and *you had better stay in bed!*"

By this time the mother was so perturbed she decided to stand unseen just outside the door to see if her sons obeyed. As she silently lurked a few feet from her chastened sons, she heard her youngest boy whisper to his older brother, "Who was that?"

Isn't it amazing? The same kids who one moment can make us red-faced with anger can in the next instant make us roar with laughter. We cherish them more than we do our own lives–even though they know exactly how to drive us batty.

But that's the deal with parenting! To be called "Mom" or "Dad" is a tremendous privilege with a corresponding challenge no less great.

The unspeakable privilege

God tells us over and over in His Word that rearing children for Him is a magnificent privilege, a blessing from heaven intended to fill our lives with joy. I have been fathering now for twenty-nine years and have more than a quarter century of experience. And yes, Donna and I have experienced both the golden moments of laughter and tender joy as well as days and nights when our hearts were heavy with anxiety and sadness.

While I don't consider myself a great father, I have learned a great many lessons. I'm now a grandpa with graying hair, and I can testify that it's crucial (as well as infinitely worth it) to start at the very beginning to influence our children for God, to make them a top priority in our lives. I'm so glad that early in the lives of my children, I decided to make my family a high priority. Never have I regretted that decision.

But it took a whack between the eyes to get me to make that choice.

A whack between the eyes

After graduating from seminary and spending two years as an apprentice, I was called to Fort Wayne, Indiana to start a church. We began with seven families meeting for worship in a mobile home. I was so excited! At last, my first pastorate!

Like most recent graduates just entering the job market, my greatest motivation in those early days was not desire, but fear–fear of failure. I remember driving around the community and thinking, *Look at all these established churches everywhere. Here I am, meeting in a cornfield in a trailer. How in the world is this ever going to work? I don't want to fail. What will all my seminary buddies say if they hear Jeremiah buried a church in a trailer in a cornfield in Indiana?*

I'd like to say I was spiritually motivated–and I hope that to some degree I was–but frankly, my primary motivator was a raging desire to avoid failure.

Even with such a tiny congregation, I never worked so hard in my life. I visited homes every night of every week, and almost the whole day on Saturdays. I even visited people in the afternoon if I could get appointments. Every Friday I organized all the contacts I had collected throughout the week, got on the phone in my tiny office, and called

> *"My BMW used to be flawless. With three kids, my Audi is anything but. Yet my life has greatly improved. God has brought more blessing into my life through these three children than any material possession ever could. Trust me. It's a lot more fun raising kids than BMWs."*
>
> **—Steve Farrar**

every name on my list to see if I could make more appointments. I did this not only to find convenient times to visit, but also because I knew I wouldn't chicken out of visiting if I held a confirmed appointment.

Week after week I kept this up. My appointment book looked like it belonged to an insurance salesman.

In the middle of this frantic activity, Donna and I were trying to rear two little children, Janice and David, just thirteen months apart. Of course, Donna was doing more of the rearing than I was. She was always at home with our kids; I never was.

Have you heard of the classic "absentee father"? That was me. Night after night I lived this frenzied lifestyle. I was trying to shepherd sheep scattered across two counties...too preoccupied to notice that a little flock under my own roof needed some shepherding too.

By the time I came home in the evenings, Donna was exhausted from caring for our little ones all day. Secretly I hoped both the children and my wife would be fast asleep by the time I rolled in. Usually we had little contact except for breakfast; then the whole cycle began again.

Eventually I started hearing some warning signals from my sweet-heart. (No doubt the signals had been sent long before, but I wasn't receiving.) Signals like this: "Are you going to be out again tonight?"

To fully appreciate Donna's dilemma you must remember that I was doing "God's work." How could she fight against the Lord? Even so, at some point she quietly but persistently began to ask that question—and a couple of times I got angry about it. "Honey," I'd lecture, "I'm the gross national product of this church. I'm it. This is all there is. I'm the staff, the secretary. If I don't do it, it's not going to be done. I've got to get out there."

And I saw the sadness in her eyes.

One morning we sat down at the kitchen table, and no matter how long I live, I'll never forget what my sweet, dear wife said to me.

"Honey," she announced, "I will never again ask you about how you spend your time. I don't know how to do that in light of what you do. But I've been praying about this, and the Lord just told me this: You are the priest of this family. These children are your responsibility. And I'm going to hold you responsible to make the right decisions."

WHAM! It's amazing the wallop a little fifteen-second speech can pack. Moments later I dropped to my knees and cried out, "God, You didn't call me to this place to destroy my family in the name of building a church. There is no conflict in Your will. I'm a father first. And if You'll help me, by the grace of God, I'll make my children the priority from this day on. They will come first."

As best as I know, from that day on my children became the priority, and I have never regretted it.

Neither will you.

A great day without regret

I don't like clichés, but the truth is, some clichés contain the gospel truth. Like the one that goes, "No one on their deathbed says, 'I wish I had spent more time at the office.'" I've never heard anyone say that, but I *have* heard a lot of people say, "I wish I'd spent more time with my children."

No doubt that truth was rattling around a lonely man's heart many years ago during the fearful days of World War II. While his son was off fighting in some far-distant corner of the world, the man sat down to compose the following anguished verses:

Dear Son,
I wish I had the power to write
The thoughts wedged in my heart tonight
As I sit watching that small star
And wondering where and how you are.
You know, Son, it's a funny thing
How close a war can really bring
A father who for years with pride
Has kept emotion deep inside.
I'm sorry, Son, when you were small
I let reserve build up that wall.
I told you, "Real men never cry."
And it was Mom who always dried
Your tears and smoothed your hurts away
So that you soon went back to play.
But, Son, deep down within my heart
I longed to have some little part

> In drying that small tear-stained face.
> But we were men. Men don't embrace.
> Suddenly I found my son
> A full grown man with childhood done.
> Tonight you're far across the sea
> Fighting away for men like me.
> Well, somehow pride and what is right
> Have somehow changed places here tonight.
> I find my eyes won't stay quite dry
> And that real men sometimes do cry.
> And if we stood here face to face,
> I'm sure, my Son, we would embrace.[1]

Our children are too precious and their time with us too short for us to neglect the unspeakable privilege we have in loving them, nurturing them, shaping them, and preparing them to step out into the wide world.

Many years ago at the high school graduation of my son, David, a moment occurred which is forever frozen in my memory. As the graduates walked up the stairs and across the stage to receive their diplomas, I leaned over and whispered in my wife's ear, "I have no regrets."

Then as now I was a busy pastor with a growing congregation and an active family. But as David took that diploma, I realized with pleasure that I hadn't missed out on his high school years. I hadn't missed any of his athletic events (OK, maybe I missed one or two). *I had been there.* As I watched my boy walk across that stage, I delighted in being able to look back and, despite all the other voices clamoring for my attention, say, "I am not sorry I said no to a lot of other things so that I could say yes to him."

If you are a parent, God has granted you the high privilege of raising a son or a daughter for Him. No matter what else you're involved in, regardless of what else you're doing, make your children a high priority. God has given you an amazing privilege! Say no to other things before you say no to your kids.

In fact, I recommend that you make it a point, every once in a while, to let your children know you have chosen them over something that is extremely important to you. Every now and then your children need to see that you have chosen to skip part of your career pursuits in order to be with them. I've tried to practice this myself.

Once I flew home from a very important meeting to attend a ball game. Another time I flew home from a strategically critical gathering to take care of a son who had busted up his ankle. I couldn't do that very often, of course, but I *had* to do it every once in a while. Why? Because I wanted each of my four children to realize, *Hey, I'm important. My parents care about me.*

And that kind of care can't dry up simply because they've left the nest. When I first came to Shadow Mountain Community Church to serve as pastor, all of my children were in school, the oldest in the eighth grade. No longer. Today my wife and I are empty-nesters. How times have changed! What *can't* change, however, what must *never* change, is my commitment to the welfare of my children. It is every bit as much a privilege to be their father today as it was when they were in diapers (maybe more so, because Grandpa doesn't have to change diapers nearly as much as Daddy did). The *nature* of my responsibility changes as my children grow up and leave home, but the *fact* of my responsibility never disappears. They'll always be my kids!

> "Caring for a family has never been easy. No one said it would be. But the price we pay to follow God's plan is worth every cost."
>
> **—Steve Farrar**

We get what we sow

Not only is it a great privilege to invest in the lives of our children, but I find it's smart to remember the rationale behind such a wise investment: We get what we sow.

Sometimes I hear parents declare that we should not try to influence our children, but rather should let them adopt their own values and form their own opinions. Secular people with whom I have debated family issues often have said to me, "You people try to force your values on your children. We believe that children ought to be allowed to choose their own values and make their own moral judgments. That way, they can grow up with a spirit of independence and be who they really are."

That may sound wise and noble, but such thinking betrays at least two fatal flaws. And the first would be reason enough to reject such thinking.

When you and I as parents refuse or neglect to teach our children values and sound moral principles, we violate clear teaching from Scripture. (And you can never, ever succeed when you walk in opposition to the declared will of God.) The New Testament reminds us fathers that we are to bring up our children in the nurture and admonition of the Lord (Ephesians 6:7). And the Old Testament, if anything, makes this even clearer. Moses tells the people of Israel:

> You shall teach them diligently to your children, and shall talk of them when you sit in your house, when you walk by the way, when you lie down, and when you rise up (Deuteronomy 6:7).

In other words, we are to dedicate our whole selves to teaching and training and forming and cultivating in the lives of our children the values which we have received from our godly forebears. So I reject the idea of letting children form their own values, because such a practice is inconsistent with the Bible, a book I hold to be supremely important.

Second, such a valueless approach to family life makes no sense. If I say I will not try to shape the values of my children, I am declaring that it is OK if anyone and anything else *does* influence and shape the way they believe and think. You say you don't want to force your views and beliefs on your children? Fine. But please don't assume that therefore they will not be influenced.

Others are dying to influence them.

If you do not influence them, someone else will. If you are not shaping their values, others will do it for you. The issue is not, *Will my child be influenced?* The issue is, *Who will be that influence?*

Most parents I know prefer to wield the greatest influence in the lives of their children. They wisely want to make the major investment in their children's lives so that the values of their offspring largely reflect their own. That's the most basic rationale for investing our life energies in the lives of our children.

We have a God-given responsibility and privilege to provide critical input for our sons and daughters, and we dare not shirk it. We are at the heart of God's training plan for the children He gives us.

A privilege to be guarded

It cannot be said too often: When God gives us children, He grants us an astonishing privilege, a blessing wholly from His loving heart of grace. That amazing truth came home to me with the power of a super-nova shortly after I accepted the pastorate at Shadow Mountain.

We thought it would be interesting to drive up into the mountains for a weekend to enjoy the snow. In the Midwest we had seen plenty of the cold, white stuff, of course, but not many Californians know about its brisk pleasures. We had been invited to spend a day at a little camp nestled in the mountains, at the former homestead of cowboy actor Tim Holt. So all six of us piled into the car and headed for a Saturday away—just the family.

As we drove higher and higher, we did indeed pass some snow. Lots of it. My children made me promise that on the way back we'd stop and play in the drifts. Finally, after rumbling over a crooked, rutted road, we found a beautiful little place filled with Shetland ponies and horses and lots of dogs. I'll never forget that day. We laughed, we ran, we played together as a family.

I think one dog almost enveloped Daniel with its unfriendly licks (at least, Daniel thought they were unfriendly). Jennifer mounted a Shetland pony, but couldn't figure out how to make it stop. I wish you could have seen her face when the pony took off! David had the opposite problem. His mount refused to budge. No matter how deep and sepul-chral my son made his voice, that horse wouldn't stir. It might as well have been a wooden horse on a carousel. And so went the day.

As we piled into the car to return home and headed back down the highway, my mind reveled in the excitement of our family excursion. There hadn't been many of them since we moved to California. As promised, on the way back we pulled off the road at a place the snow piled high along the highway. Before anyone got out of the car I gave clear instructions to the whole family: "Whatever you do, stay on the *passenger* side of the car. Don't you dare get over on the driver's side! Get as far away from the road as you can."

I hadn't taken two steps out of the car when David hit me square in the back of the head with an ice-ball. Of course, I had to retaliate. Immediately I forgot all about the rest of the family and took off after him. Twenty yards from the car, I heard a horn blaring. I turned around just in time to see Jennifer, not ten minutes out of the car, walking around to the driver's side, right next to the road–as a truck roared down the highway in her direction.

Now, if you've driven in the mountains, you know truckers use gravity to their advantage. That truck was flying.

Terrified, I sprinted toward my daughter and yanked her back to the safe side of the car. Next I administered a reminder to her backside so she wouldn't disobey me again. Last I hugged her, and we all got back in the car and started home.

All was quiet driving down the mountain, except for an occasional, "sniff, sniff" from the back seat. "Jennifer," I said at last, "I want you to climb over the seat and sit on my lap." She didn't want to, but I insisted. "Do it anyway," I instructed.

Donna and I have always tried to express our love to our children right after administering discipline, so right there in the car I hugged my daughter up against me and said, "Honey, I love you and you scared me. I wouldn't want anything ever to happen to you."

And then–I don't know how to explain it–I lost it. I started to cry.

The tears rushed to my eyes with such force that I could barely see the road. I had to stop the car, pull off the highway, and wipe my eyes. And I remember thinking, *Why am I crying? She got the spanking, not me.*

Gradually it began to dawn on me that much more was wrapped up in our frightening moment than it first appeared. A montage of pictures sprang to life: a family desperate for time away; the fresh excitement of a glorious day totally committed to each other with no interruptions; the fun of a mom and dad and sisters and brothers playing contentedly together; and yes, the cold fear of losing someone I dearly love. Every parent knows the terror prompted by the mere thought of losing a child. The very idea strikes a sword deep into your heart.

At that moment, as these thoughts coalesced in my mind, I began to ponder one more notion–namely, how important it was that my children have more of their father than they were getting.

It was yet another solid whack between the eyes administered by a gracious Heavenly Father.

Have similar thoughts ever crossed your mind? I wonder–why does it so often take a traumatic experience to show us the priceless treasures that are our children? All of us need to laugh with our kids at the crazy things that are a part of growing up. And all of us, if we work at it, can dream up fun things to do that will inject some relief and laughter and humor back into the pressure cooker our kids call their world.

They're worth it, you know. Every bit of it. They're God's good gift to us, and it's our inestimable privilege to help them grow up under our roofs. Oh, friend, let's make sure we make the most of the opportunity!

The daunting challenge

Don't get me wrong! Rearing families in this generation is no easy thing, no carefree stroll in the park. We are living in what has been called "a toxic environment," and all parents, regardless of their children's ages, endure sleepless nights and anxious days over the fate of the precious ones God has put into their hands.

Sometimes all of us have felt like taking the advice of Mark Twain, who suggested a novel idea of rearing children. On one occasion he wrote:

> Things run along pretty smoothly until your kid reaches thirteen. That's the time you need to stick 'em in a barrel, hammer the lid down nice and snug, and feed 'em through the knothole. And then, about the time he turns sixteen, *plug up the knothole!*[2]

What parent hasn't at one time or another entertained thoughts along these lines? Of course, I don't recommend this method as the ideal way to deal with the challenges of parenting!

Stewards, not owners

One of the biggest challenges facing us as parents is the necessity of giving our children back to the God who created them. While we are highly privileged to bring up children in the nurture and admonition of the Lord, we must remember that we do not own them.

The Lord says, "For every living soul belongs to me, the father as well as the son–both alike belong to me" (Ezekiel 18:4, NIV).

Our children are not our possessions; they belong to God. We are merely stewards of their tender souls for a short time—basically, for twenty years. We are wise if we give them back to God when He gives them to us. Then we will be able to enjoy them as ours in a way impossible otherwise.

A.W. Tozer once wrote, "Everything in life which we commit to God is really safe. And everything which we refuse to commit to Him is never safe."[3] If we enter parenthood realizing that God has given us a great gift, an opportunity to be a steward over a child for approximately a fourth to a third of his or her life, then even as we begin the task of parenting we will understand that the day soon comes when we shall move through this passageway on to other things. Really, this is the only way to parent effectively.

Do you remember the story of Hannah in the Old Testament? In 1 Samuel 1:1-28 we meet an anxious Hannah, distraught because her husband had failed to give her a child. The Bible pointedly says that the Lord had "kept" her from childbearing.

In the midst of her distress she visited the priest, Eli. Eli mistook her anguish for drunkenness and rebuked her for it. But when this desperate woman poured out to him the sorrow of her heart, Eli told her that God would grant her request.

"If I have a son from God," Hannah replied, "I will give him back to Him." First Samuel 1:11 puts it like this: "I will give him to the LORD all the days of his life." And Hannah was true to her word. When the child Samuel was born, she took him to Eli and said, "So I have also dedicated him to the LORD; as long as he lives he is dedicated to the LORD" (NASB). From the very beginning, Hannah understood (better than many of us do) that her son belonged to God.

How do we present our children to the Lord? Hannah gave Samuel to the priest, but in our day that is unnecessary; we do not need to deposit our children at the doorstep of the church. God no longer lives in a tabernacle or temple as He did in Old Testament times. Instead He takes up residence in our hearts when through faith we give our lives to Jesus Christ. The blessed New Covenant grants that our sons and daughters may remain under our own roofs even as we give our children back to God. Yet in both the Old and the New Testaments the critical point remains the same: Our children belong to God. We simply serve as stewards of their growing-up years.

I think that's what God was getting at when He took Abraham and Isaac up Mount Moriah (Genesis 22). The Lord wanted to find out the extent of Abraham's commitment to Him. Was he more committed to God than he was to his own son, the son of promise?

While the Lord probably will not bring us to a literal Mount Moriah, He does insist that we answer the same question He posed to Abraham. Are we more committed to God than we are even to our own children? Do we understand that we do not own them, but that they belong to God? Are we willing to face the implications that we are stewards, not possessors?

One of the hardest things we parents must face is that the little one we hold in our arms doesn't truly belong to us. He or she belongs to God alone. The Lord has given that child to us for a period of time to influence, to encourage, to guide, and to direct. If in the very beginning we give that child back to God, it will be easier for us on the day—much sooner than we imagine—that son or daughter will leave our home and move on to another chapter in his or her life.

Loving in the hard times

God has called us to love our children, but loving them doesn't mean it always comes naturally. Loving them means that no matter what they are, what they do, where they go, they're still ours. Sometimes love is tough to express—but it's still necessary. A story that came across the Internet illustrates the point:

Some time ago, a father punished his three-year-old daughter for wasting a roll of gold wrapping paper. Money was tight, and he became infuriated when the child tried to decorate a box to put under the tree. Nevertheless, the little girl brought the gift to her father the next morning and said, "This is for you, Daddy." He was embarrassed by his earlier overreaction, but his anger flared again when he found that the box was empty.

He yelled at her, "Don't you know that when you give someone a present, there's supposed to be something inside of it?"

The little girl looked up at him with tears in her eyes and said, "Oh, Daddy, it's not empty. I blew kisses into the box. All for you, Daddy."

The father was crushed. He put his arms around his little girl and begged her forgiveness. He kept that gold box by his bed for years. Whenever he was discouraged, he would take out an imaginary kiss and remember the love of the child who had put it there.

As believers in Jesus Christ, as men and women filled with the indwelling Spirit of God, you and I have the capacity to love without restraints or conditions. It is the supernatural love of God flowing through our weakness and human inability.

And let's face it, it's not always easy to love our children. Scripture tells us that real love–the genuine article–"bears all things, believes all things, hopes all things, endures all things. Love never fails" (1 Corinthians 13:7-8). That kind of love doesn't flow naturally from this man's heart. But our God is an overflowing fountain of love, a rushing river of love, a vast ocean of love without bottom and without shore. And if we belong to Him, that divine love can pour over the spillways of our lives.

Even when it's tough.

Sometimes it's a war

Let's be honest. Parenting can be a war. One author put it this way:

Every baby starts life as a little savage. He is completely selfish and self-centered. He wants what he wants when he wants it: his bottle, his mother's attention, his playmate's toy, his uncle's watch. Deny these and he seethes with rage and aggressiveness which would be murderous were he not so helpless. This means that all children, not just certain children, are born delinquent. If permitted to continue in the self-centered world of infancy, given free rein to his impulsive actions, every child would grow up a criminal, a thief, a killer, a rapist.[4]

Parenting can be a war because children are naturally self-centered. If you don't believe that, go to the shopping mall this afternoon. I was there recently and walked by a mother with a little tot trailing behind her, screaming his lungs out. Obviously he had been denied something he wanted. I finished making my purchases, then walked by that same mother and child twenty-five minutes later. He was still screaming at the top of his lungs. Not once had he stopped in all that time; his voice remained as strong and lusty as ever. He wanted his way.

Those of us with years of parenting experience know there is a way to deal with such an outburst, but obviously that young mother hadn't yet learned. Perhaps she was a "modern mother" who felt the child should be allowed to express himself. In a mall, bystanders can endure it because they can walk away. But it's a different story on a plane.

I seem to get them every time I fly…expressing themselves to the limit of their ability. I confess to the most ungodly thoughts as I sit there, strapped down thirty thousand feet in the air, while some aggrieved little one howls and screeches and bellows out his discontent. I feel sorry for the poor parents who must deal with that (and I pray for the flight attendants).

Parenting can be a war, a war between two wills, the will of the parent and the will of the child. When they are infants we tend to pass over it. And many parents today are deathly afraid of laying a finger on their children in public for fear they will be arrested for child abuse.

It gets really tough when those children who have been allowed to express themselves without restraint get to be thirteen, fourteen, or fifteen years old. They have learned that if they insist on whatever they want, they get their way. It's become a pattern by that point.

It may also become a tragedy.

Some time ago I was reading Malachi 4:5-6 and noticed something that had previously escaped my attention. Malachi wrote concerning the coming of the Lord:

> Behold, I will send you Elijah the prophet
> Before the coming of the great and dreadful day of the LORD.
> And he will turn
> The hearts of the fathers to the children,
> And the hearts of the children to their fathers,
> Lest I come and strike the earth with a curse.

As we move toward the end of the age when Christ will return, the hearts of the fathers *won't* be toward their children and the hearts of the children *won't* be toward their fathers. A war will rage between parents and children. Even now we may be living in the dawn of that time. The Apostle Paul predicted that in the end times children will be disobedient to their parents (2 Timothy 3:2).

The Bible never says that parenting is easy, a constant thrill with unending exhilaration, one grand party. Sometimes it's far from that. Sometimes, it's a battle royal. Our children don't always want the same things we want. Challenges present themselves everywhere we go.

Yet we can win this war if we are God's people. We have every reason to be men and women of hope, of confidence, of optimism. Why? Because we do not fight this battle alone. Parenting presents great challenges, yes, but Christians can plug into the almighty Power that flung the universe into being. That very power is available to us to build our homes on a solid foundation that can withstand any of the dark forces arrayed against us.

Faith is the key

There is no such thing as painless parenting. Pain—even excruciating pain—is a natural part of the family process in our broken world. Women know better than anyone that *pain* is how the family got started. And the aches and pangs, the hurts and hassles will continue to intrude into the parenting pathway through the years, whether we like it or not.

That's why a vital faith in Jesus Christ is so crucial to a happy family. Frankly, I don't know how families without a faith in God make it. I can't imagine how they survive. How blessed we are that God equips us through faith to meet all the challenges of parenting, even parenting in a toxic environment!

Observe the instructions to families in the Bible and you will notice one recurrent theme. Consider Ephesians 6:1, for example. "Children, obey your parents." How? "In the Lord." Or read Ephesians 5:25: "Husbands, love your wives." How? "As Christ loved the church." Or Ephesians 5:22: "Wives, be submissive to your husband." How? "As to the Lord." All these instructions to the family wrap around

> *"You can do it. That's right. You can really do it. Not you in general, but you specifically. You, the person reading these words, can accomplish what many of the 'notables' of our day and of history have failed to accomplish. In the midst of a very evil age, you can parent godly children."*
>
> **—James R. Lucas**

a core of faith in God and Jesus Christ.

Don't try to build your family without faith in God, unless you like feeling frustrated, miserable, and hopeless. You face an awesome task in building and leading your family, and you desperately need God to help you. Throw yourself on His grace and mercy and say to Him, "Lord, I'm a flawed human being and I know that apart from You, I can't do anything but mess this thing up. So I'm going to hang on to You with both hands. Together, we'll make this family work."

And how does God feel about such prayers? Hear it from our Lord's own lips: "For whoever exalts himself will be humbled, and he who humbles himself will be exalted" (Luke 14:11).

You *can* make your family "work." *Your* family can become a beacon of light, reaching out in the darkness of these uncertain days to give others the same hope in Christ you enjoy. Through a living faith in an omnipotent, loving God, it's not only possible...it's your destiny!

Today is a good day

Don't allow the very real challenges of parenting to dismay your soul or crush your spirit. One tired wife and mother who died in 1860 left this testament to the world as an epitaph on her tombstone:

> Here lies a poor woman who was always tired,
> for she lived in a place where help wasn't hired.
> Her last words on earth were, "Friends, I am going
> where washing ain't done, nor sweeping, nor sewing,
> and everything there is exact to my wishes,
> for there they don't eat and there's no washing of dishes.
> Don't mourn for me now.
> Don't mourn for me never,
> for I'm going to do nothing
> for ever and ever.

We don't have to wait for the glories of heaven to enjoy life. By God's grace, we can taste a bit of heaven even now, in our homes. Our Lord has called us and enabled us to serve as His stewards over the lives of the children He has placed under our roofs, and it is our great privilege to rear them for His glory.

I love a song Bill and Gloria Gaither wrote many years ago. Apparently a lot of others enjoy it, too, for the song has been recorded many times by various groups. The song's lyrics remain deeply special to me:

> Hold tight to the sound of the music of living;
> Happy songs from the laughter of children at play.
> Hold my hand as we run through the sweet, fragrant
>   meadows,
> Making memories of what was today.
> Tiny voice that I hear as my little girl calling
> For Daddy to hear just what she has to say,
> My little son running there by the hillside,
> May never be quite like today.
> We have this moment to hold in our hand,
> And to touch as it slips through our fingers like sand.
> Yesterday's gone, and tomorrow may never come,
> But we have these moments, today.[5]

Today is the best day to love our children.

Today is the right day to cherish them, nurture them, train them, and prepare them to leave our home and build a family of their own.

Make no mistake, this is a high privilege that comes with great challenges and even greater rewards. And best of all, *you can do it!* God has called you into partnership with Himself in the creation of a loving Christian home, and *His* partnerships—whacks on the head included—have a knack for spectacular success.

1 James S. Hewett, Editor, *Illustrations Unlimited* (Wheaton, Ill.: Tyndale House Publishers, Inc., 1988), 200-201.

2 Charles R. Swindoll, *Growing Wise in Family Life* (Portland, Ore.: Multnomah Press, 1988), 87.

3 A.W. Tozer, *The Pursuit of God*, special ed. (Wheaton, Ill.: Tyndale Publishing House, n.d.), 28.

4 *Minnesota Crime Commission Report* cited in Charles R. Swindoll, *Growing Wise in Family Life*, (Portland, Ore.: Multnomah Press, 1988), 102.

5 Bill and Gloria Gaither, "This Moment Today," used by permission.

two

Children: One of God's
Best Gifts

"A baby is a small member of the home

that makes love stronger, days shorter, nights longer,

the bank roll smaller, the home happier,

the clothes shabbier, the past forgotten,

and the future worth living for."

—LAURENS VAN DER POST AND JANE TAYLOR

*t*here is joy, great joy, in children! I know that may be hard to remember when you have little ones at home who keep you up all night, but it's true. Children are meant by Almighty God to be tremendous sources of blessing.

In fact, God sees the children He gives us as benedictions and graces to life. Over and over the Word of God makes a special point to proclaim the beauty and the blessing and the joy of children. Consider just four examples:

> He grants the barren woman a home,
> Like a joyful mother of children.
> Praise the LORD!
> (Psalm 113:9)

> Behold, children are a heritage from the LORD,
> The fruit of the womb is a reward
> (Psalm 127:3).

> Like arrows in the hand of a warrior,
> So are the children of one's youth.
> Happy is the man who has his quiver full of them;
> They shall not be ashamed,
> But shall speak with their enemies in the gate
> (Psalm 127:4-5).

> The father of the righteous will greatly rejoice.
> And he who begets a wise child will delight in him.
> Let your father and your mother be glad.
> And let her who bore you rejoice
> (Proverbs 23:24-25).

Jewish people of the Old Testament, and some of our Jewish friends of today, have the most positive concept of the family, a concept which came to them out of the Old Testament Scriptures.

Joy from heaven

Scarcely do you get inside the cover of the Bible before you read that at the birth of Cain, Eve declared she had received her son from the Lord (Genesis 4:1). Just a few chapters later, Abraham heard that God was going to open Sarah's womb even in old age, and she would receive a child from the Lord. God took pity on Leah, we are told, and opened her womb (Genesis 29:31). He did the same thing for Rachel (Genesis 30:22). And we read that the Lord gave Ruth conception (Ruth 4:13).

> "The Psalms call children a 'reward.' Not a curse, not a tragedy, not an accident—they are the expression of God's favor. It is a thrilling sight to see your children through the lens of Scripture as His trophies."
>
> **—Howard Hendricks**

It is the Lord who honors the marriage bed and the process of childbearing and it is He who brings about the miracle of birth.

Donna and I were married about five-and-a-half years before we had any children. Noting our childless condition, some godly women from the church where I first served on staff took it upon themselves to pray for us. It wasn't so bad that they prayed, but periodically they would want to hear a "report" on how their prayers were doing. That was a little embarrassing. After our third child came along as a result of their prayers, we actually made a long distance call and asked them to cease and desist–at least for a while.

The truth of the Word of Almighty God is that children come as a result of God's blessing upon us. If you have ever been present at the birth of a child, you know the event cannot be explained in human terms. Nothing I know of comes close to the look on the face of a new mother. A special kind of glow, a unique shimmer of godliness, lights up her countenance, especially if she knows the Lord and understands that her child is a gift from God. Such a mother wears joy all over her face. You walk into the hospital room where a new mom is nursing her baby and you feel as though you're stepping on holy ground.

Children are a loan to us from God–you might say, God's home improvement loan. Any child who is nurtured and loved as God wants him to be *will* improve his home. The greatest lessons to be learned about life, love, purpose, meaning, and priority are to be learned from children. God gave them to us not merely so we could love, nurture, and teach *them*, but so they in turn could be God's teachers to *us*. They teach us what sacrificial love is about, what it means to put somebody else first when it is hard to do it, and how to love with God's *agape* love.

A friend of mine suffered from periodic bouts of depression that would all but immobilize him. He tells how his little girl, six or seven at the time, would come out to the backyard in the summer and lay down beside him on the lawn. She wouldn't say a word; she just wanted to be there with him.

How we should thank God for the gift of children!

Teach them that they're special

Our children need to hear from us how special they are, and they need to hear it in terms they both understand and believe. I doubt you can do anything greater for your children than to let them know you believe in them. Our kids need to know beyond a shadow of a doubt that we believe in them and are there to support and encourage them.

An old story says that the sculptor Michelangelo was pushing a huge piece of rock down the street one day. A curious neighbor poked his head out of a window and asked, "Why are you straining over that old beat-up piece of rock?" And Michelangelo replied, "Because there's an angel in that rock who's trying to get out!"

Similarly, there are special people in our kids who are trying to get out. And they *will* get out when we encourage them and make them know we're on their team. Sure, they'll blow it; but so will we! We need to be their most eager cheerleaders and their most loyal champions.

Author David Ferguson has come to know how priceless are the gifts of his children. He writes:

> The depth of our friendship and intimacy with each of our children is a source of blessing that has empowered our ministry to others. Countless times during the stress and overload of ministry God has enriched us and rekindled our zeal through one of our "rewards"–Terri, Robin, or Eric. During a stress-filled day at the office, I often

focus on one of the many family pictures in my office. As I pause to remember a time of family blessing, God rekindles a heart of gratefulness for our children.

One Saturday afternoon Teresa and I were driving home from a week of ministering to Christian leadership couples in crisis. Our son, Eric, who was in his early twenties at the time, called on the mobile phone, and Teresa answered.

"Hi Mom," he said. "What are you and Dad doing?"

"We're on our way home," she said.

"What are your plans tonight?" Eric pressed.

We were silent for several seconds. Exhausted from an intensive week of ministry and teaching, we had no plans, and we didn't want any plans. But Eric obviously had an agenda.

"No plans, Eric," Teresa said. "We're just going home."

Eric presented his request. He wanted to know if he and his girlfriend could come to our house and play games with us. We were silent again, then the blessing came: Our young adult son wanted to bring his girlfriend over to spend time with us. This kind of stress we can manage! The joy of the Lord was our strength that night as we treasured the relationship with our son.

Robin and her husband, Ike, bless us daily with their choice to work with us full-time in our ministry, enriching thousands of church leaders with their support and caring concern.

Terri, our oldest, recently brought into our lives the special blessing of Wayne, her new husband. Wayne had been widowed with two precious sons, Brad and Michael. We not only have a new son, we also have instant grandsons to multiply our blessing. Our reward from the Lord continues to grow.[1]

The Bible insists that the little ones we have in our homes (Psalm 128 calls them "olive plants") are from God. Children are not accidents that come to derail our career plans. They are not inconveniences or intrusions into the lives of busy parents. Our children are God's gifts to us.

Ten ways to love your kids

So what are we to do once we understand that our children are God's benediction lovingly bestowed on our homes? We love them! And how do we do that? Allow me to make ten suggestions for communicating love to our children.

1. Establish boundaries for their lives.

If you talked to as many young people as I do, you would soon discover that most who grow up in homes without boundaries or restrictions would give anything for some tangible evidence that Mom and Dad care enough to insist on knowing where their kids are and what they are doing. Boundaries are critical if we're to communicate love to our children.

When David was in the sixth grade, his basketball team lacked a coach and somehow I was asked to take on the job. I agreed, then went out and recruited former NBA center Swen Nater to help me. What a delightful experience! We had some good athletes, the team played well, and we won most of our games.

One day when I picked up David at school to take him to a game, I noticed a sheepish look on his face. What was wrong? I discovered he had gotten into trouble at school that day—in his principal's words, "He has been a bit belligerent."

Normally David did a good job of respecting his elders, so I did a little more checking and discovered that one of his teammates came to school that day without his uniform and shoes. He didn't have time to go home and get them before the game, so he tried to call his parents. He walked to the school's business office to make the call, but a school rule prohibited students from using its phone to make personal calls. David could not understand why the rule couldn't be relaxed for something as vital as the ball game, and he expressed his opinion strenuously.

When we hopped in the car and headed to the game, I had to explain that he had behaved unacceptably. Our family held to a boundary that said we respect our elders, even if we think they are wrong.

I knew I had to respond to his belligerent behavior and I also knew what that response must be–David would not be allowed to start the game or play the first few minutes. I remember sitting on the bench, choking back tears, knowing that I had hurt my son in a place he couldn't be hurt any more deeply. But this message had to be sent. When at last I told David his time was up, you never saw anybody check into a game as fast as he did that day.

We discover how firm our boundaries really are only after they've been tested. But by setting boundaries for our children, we convey our love for them. In essence we say to them, "I love you too much to let you grow up in any other way than the way I know will honor God and bless you."

Psychologist Joyce Brothers once wrote, "Strictness has been considered an old-fashioned method of parenting, but it may be coming back into style. A recent study of almost two thousand fifth and sixth graders, some of whom have been reared by strict parents, others by permissive ones, produced some surprising results. The children who had been strictly disciplined possessed high self-esteem, were high achievers socially and academically. What these children said revealed that they were actually happier than the undisciplined children; they loved the adults who made and enforced the rules they lived by."[2]

Dr. Brothers is absolutely on target! If we are to love our children, we need to communicate that love by caring enough to build some fences around them.

2. Enjoy them.

It's *fun* to have kids.

It seems strange to have to write that statement, but so many negative, caustic voices say the opposite that I feel I must.

When our daughter Jan left for school, do you know what I missed the most? Her laugh. She has the most infectious laugh and she finds humor in things nobody else finds funny. But when she laughs, all the rest of us roar with her. It's such a joy for laughter to fill the home.

When we first came to California, we were quickly introduced to its culture. One of our great surprises? The way friends convey love to you.

You know you've made it with your peers when every night they start to decorate your home with toilet paper. Our trees have seen more TP than any in El Cajon, I guarantee you. Dozens of times we have awakened and looked out the window to see that it does indeed snow in California.

After these artificial snowfalls occurred about ten times in a row—the last one followed by a good rain shower—we decided to find out who was so regularly expressing their love. We discovered a little girl named Courtney was behind all of this, so I told my son and his friends that it was time to get even.

One fateful night we executed a well-planned operation. The boys loaded up my van with *seventy-two* rolls of the finest TP you've ever seen. I was the "wheel man." We drove to Courtney's home and covered her front yard with paper—a masterful job! We set up a signal system so that if I saw anyone coming, I'd beep twice on the horn, they'd scramble in the van, and we were gone. I couldn't help but wonder what would have happened had our Chairman of the Board of Deacons seen me wheeling out of that neighborhood with a handful of wild-eyed young men. (By the way, back when this happened, David was young and this was innocent fun. Now, in some places, it is against the law.)

I can't imagine families growing up without smiles or laughter or craziness. It's one of the ways we say to our kids, "You're important." "We love you." "It's fun being with you." "Is this a great family God has given us, or what?"

3. Expose our humanness to them.

Our kids need to hear us say, "I'm sorry, I blew it," when we make a mistake. Whether you have one child or fourteen, it is impossible to get them all the way from the cradle through graduation without making a serious mistake for which you will have to apologize. Who among us hasn't spanked the wrong kid? Or blown up before we knew the facts?

One day at five in the afternoon, my daughter Jan came tooling into the living room and announced, "Daddy, I have to get something at the mall." A church board meeting had been scheduled that night for 7 o'clock.

"Now?" I said. I needn't have asked; she always had to have it now.

"Could you take me?" she pleaded.

"Well, sure," I replied, "but honey, I'm on a short leash tonight. I've got to be at a board meeting at seven, so we can't stay very long."

"That's fine," she said.

Now, Jan is a committed shopper; she has the spiritual gift of shopping. I hate it, but I've learned to do it because it's something she loves to do. Before she went off down the mall, I instructed her, "Don't forget, we have to leave the shopping center no later than 6:30."

"OK, I'll be back by 6:30," she agreed as she left me to putter around the Walden bookstore (in my mind, the only redemptive place in the whole outfit).

A half-hour later I sat down on a bench. It was 6:10 and I waited for the next twenty minutes. Six-thirty came, but Jan didn't. Six-thirty-five, still no Jan. Six-forty, no sign of her. I stared at my watch, realizing I'd be late for the meeting. Already I had forfeited dinner. Six-forty-five, she hadn't come along. Six-fifty, still no Jan. Finally, at seven minutes till seven, I looked up and there she was, strolling down the mall as if time were of no concern. She wore a big smile and carried a bag stuffed with purchases. She walked up to me as if nothing were wrong–and I could feel the blood pulsating in my neck.

I had already prepared the speech–a rare speech, one of my better ones. And when I saw my daughter, I made the biggest mistake we parents make. I asked for no information, I simply made all the assumptions and convicted her without a trial.

"I can't imagine that after I went out of my way to bring you here…." I began, then paused. "You've returned now almost a half-hour late. I'm going to be late for my meeting. I just can't imagine you being so insensitive! Jan, do you have a conscience?"

She didn't say a word. We walked briskly and silently to the van, got in, and she started to cry. "What are you crying about?" I demanded.

"Dad," she said, "my watch broke."

"Oh, come on–you can come up with a better one than that!" I chided.

The van went quiet again, except for her sniffling. When we arrived home and walked into the house, Donna asked, "Why are you so late?"

"Honey," I said, "you aren't gonna believe this," and I recounted what had happened and what Jan had said.

Donna looked at me and stated matter-of-factly, "Dave, her watch *is* broken. It has been acting strangely, it stops intermittently, and we don't know what's wrong. We were going to take it in and get it repaired tomorrow."

Gulp. I heard my daughter sniffling in her bedroom and penitently made my way to her door, then knocked.

"May I come in?" I asked quietly.

"Yes," she said.

"Honey, I am so sorry," I began. "I have blown it so bad. I didn't even ask you. I didn't know about your watch. Can you ever forgive me? Please forgive me for the things I said—they were totally unwarranted."

Jan looked up and said through tears, "Sure, Dad, everybody makes mistakes." We held each other for a few minutes, I went on to my meeting, and life continued.

When we've been wrong, we communicate love to our children by admitting our human inadequacies face-to-face. In the process, we teach them how to follow our example as they grow older.

4. Explain the reasons behind our decisions.

In my opinion, "Because I said so" ought to be stricken from every parent's vocabulary. What worthless words! Our children deserve the recognition and treatment appropriate to growing adults. It should be our goal to help them reason through our decisions. That doesn't mean they will always accept our judgments, of course, but at least they need to understand the rationale behind those decisions.

One day Jan came home and wanted to know if she could attend a certain movie with her friends. "No," I said. Why not? she wanted to know. "Give me the evening to think about it and I'll tell you tomorrow," I replied.

The next day I was as honest as I could be. "Honey," I said, "that's a door that's never been opened in your life, and if I say yes to you today, I have opened that door. I can't emotionally do it, because I know that if I open it, I can never close it. Maybe I will open it someday; maybe I'll deal with it in a different way tomorrow. But for right now, here's the reason I said no: I just can't emotionally deal with opening that door in your life, so I won't."

"OK," she said, and that was it. I never heard about it again.

Sometimes we sell our kids short. We don't think they can deal with our reasons and we aren't willing to admit that sometimes our reasons dwell within us. Our kids deserve to know our reasons, whatever they are.

5. Exchange ideas with them.

Our children will know they're something special when we take the time to exchange ideas with them. When we expose them to an intellectual life beyond the routines of a busy household, they will see we are treating them as valuable people. And many times they grasp more from these exchanges than we suppose.

A young father regularly read stories out of a children's Bible to his three-year-old son. Now, this little boy had a mind of his own and often had to take "time-outs" for misbehavior. One day this father read to his boy the story of Jonah and the great fish. At the end of the story, after hearing how the disobedient prophet had been swallowed and three days later spit out on shore, the father asked, "What happened to Jonah?" The little boy thought for a moment and then replied, "God had to give him a time-out." Bingo!

Our children need to verbally interact with their parents on issues other than discipline, clothes, food, and other mundane things. They will know they are loved when we make the effort to develop their minds through the stimulating exchange of ideas.

6. Encourage them.

The commitment to encourage our children may be the most important lesson this generation can learn. Encouragement in regular and massive doses is probably the best thing we can give our kids to help them know we are on their team.

Somebody has said that encouragement is the nutrition on which our spirits thrive. We need to be cheerleaders for our kids, their number-one fans, helping them to believe in themselves because they know we believe in them. They need to know that we'd break our necks to do whatever we have to do to help them feel special.

I know my mom thought I was the greatest, even though I knew better. She never missed any event in which I had a part and she constantly reinforced in me the idea that I could be better than I thought I was. And that confidence can never, ever be overthrown, no matter how long you live.

When David was a freshman in high school, he and one other freshman made the varsity basketball team. David was the youngest guy on the team that year, and they had a good team.

We played Grossmont the first game of the year. David was so psyched up, he didn't touch the ground—so pumped that he did everything wrong. He even shot an air ball. An air ball is a shot that doesn't hit anything—not the iron, not the backboard, not the net, not anything. Nothing but air. It usually prompts the opposing crowd to chant a two-note cheer, "Aaaaaair-ball! Aaaaaair-ball! Aaaaair…," every time the hapless player touches the ball. It's the most awful sound a basketball player can hear.

Now, everyone who plays basketball shoots an air ball at some point. Larry Bird shot air balls. Magic Johnson shot air balls. Even Michael Jordan occasionally shot air balls. But when you're a high-school freshman who's trying to achieve and you shoot an air ball, it's devastating.

After the final buzzer, I had one discouraged young man on my hands. I didn't know how to pump him back up. The next day at work I fussed over how to encourage my son. So I sat down at my computer and wrote a long letter to him.

In the letter I tried to tell David, "Hey, it's the first game you've ever played in high school. You're a freshman, but you're playing varsity. You play in the best league in the eighth largest city in America!" (I found out later my facts were wrong

"If God blesses you with children, you'll be taking part in one of the most significant accomplishments a man can enjoy. Some guys head their own corporations by age thirty-five. Big deal. Some guys win five gold medals at the Olympics. Big deal. Some guys climb Mount Everest. Big deal. Some guys swim the length of the Pacific under water without taking a breath. Big deal. In my book, none of those exploits come close to the man who has learned to change a dirty diaper without throwing up. That's what I call a big deal. Especially when you can do it without an oxygen mask."

—Steve Farrar

on the size of San Diego, but that misses the point.)

I did everything I could think of to encourage him. I told him he was just getting started, but that if he kept plugging, he could be a great basketball player. I made a list of all the good things he had done, as well as all the things he needed to work on. I wanted him to know that, in my mind, he was "all-world."

We need to keep searching for opportunities to encourage our kids. They need it so much. Authors Gary Smalley and John Trent once advised that all our criticism of our kids ought to be like a thin slice of meat in a sandwich, encompassed by thick slices of bread. The bread is praise and encouragement which ought to both precede and follow any critical remarks.

7. Help them to believe they can go further than they dream.

Our job as parents is to let our kids know they can be better than they ever hope to be. If they're getting B's, we can find positive ways to convince them they probably could earn A's. If they're scoring fifteen points a game, perhaps we can broaden their horizons to hope that they might be able to score eighteen.

God invites us to challenge our sons and daughters to look beyond where they are now to imagine a broader and richer and greater future. We can help promote in them a sense that they can achieve the greatest possible good in their lives.

8. Physically express what we feel in our hearts.

Most of us fathers find it easy to hug our little girls, but as they get older and begin to develop as women, it becomes more difficult—even though that's when our daughters need it the most. Yet we can work through this. Our grown daughters need to know the physical affection of their fathers.

And there's nothing wrong with fathers hugging their sons, either! In a column titled "Four hugs a day—chase the blues away," a newspaper columnist wrote, "I suspect society at large suffers from low-grade chronic hug deficiency, and we don't even know it."[5] I think he's right. A hug says something that cannot be communicated in any other way.

For many years now I've kept in my files a faded reproduction of a moving parable titled "A Certain Man, a Little Girl, and a Horse," written by a pastor and delivered for the first time at the Yale School of Divinity. More than anything I have ever heard, it expresses the importance of drawing so near to our children that our love can be tangibly felt. For the only kind of love we can use is the love that we feel.

There was a certain middle-class suburban pastor who lived with his little girl in a seven-room parsonage. When the girl was only four-years-old, her mother died, and after that the little girl was unusually sad. She seldom smiled or laughed; never put her arms around anyone; played alone in her room for hours on end; and talked quietly to herself as she fell asleep each night. No matter how bright the sun shone in the morning, at breakfast in that parsonage a gloomy little voice would report, "I feel sad, I always feel sad. Daddy, you know that, so why do you always ask? I wish I could be born all over again."

Accompanying the sadness of this little girl was her insatiable desire to own a horse; not a hobby horse, or a stuffed horse, or the kind of horse you pull across the floor with a string, but a real-live-horse. And she couldn't seem to get it through her head that there was no way to house a horse in the parsonage. She only felt that it would fill some of the emptiness that she was too young to describe.

When the little girl's mother had become seriously ill, everyone was brave about it and they put on their very Christian face and they never cried around the little girl. Everyone talked about how happy a place Heaven was and told her that her mommy wouldn't hurt anymore. Her father thought that was the sensible way to handle the whole affair. Mommy had been very courageous too, and part of her courage through her long and painful illness had been to help the little girl become accustomed to getting along without her, so as

soon as she knew she was going to die, she began invit-
ing different friends and nursemaids to take the little girl
on holidays and for long weekends.

Her mother had really wanted to gather her daughter in her arms and laugh and cry with her to tell her
how much she loved her, but she had known she would
soon be leaving this world and thought the least she
could do was allow the child's attachment not to grow
too strong. And so she finally died, leaving husband and
child to comfort each other the best they could.

The little girl's father tried to be affectionate but she
was not normally a very loving child, and he thought
he was being sensible not to force himself on her—after
all, she squirmed and complained that his whiskers
scratched when he kissed her, so he gave that up too.

All of this happened before one particular night
when the pastor was very wearily putting his little girl
to bed. Although she was in one of her uncooperative
moods, she finally got tucked in and he knelt down to
hear her prayers. As usual, they were very proper
prayers: "Now I lay me down to sleep…."

But on this night, the tragic dimension of the child
took over. She launched out on her own, apart from the
memorized prayer, and she began to plead, "Dear God,
help me not to feel so sad all the time."

Her father felt a tear in his eye and another one
rolled down his cheek, and he was very alarmed, for he
thought, *If she knows I'm crying, her world will surely tumble
in. I must be composed and sure for her—but it was too late.* A
tear once shed cannot be recalled, and one had, quite
out of control, fallen on the child's face deep in her
cuddly blanket.

"Daddy, you're crying," she said.

"Oh no, my dear," came the false assurance. "Go to
sleep now, pleasant dreams."

"But you *are* crying," she said, not with alarm but

with curiosity.

And he could not pose any longer–after all, he was a pastor and he had some respect for the truth. "Well, just a tear or two tonight," he said. And then, with almost angry self-assertion, he added, "It's just possible you know that Daddy feels sad sometimes, too."

"You do?" she paused. "What about? Mommy?"

"Yes, about Mommy. Sometimes I miss her very much."

"Is that what you're crying about tonight?"

"No dear," he said, almost before he realized what he was doing. "Tonight I feel sad about you, about your feeling so sad. I love you so very much that it hurts, it hurts awfully that you are so sad," and then he paused– he had said too much. How could he repair the damage to her security?

The silence between them was awkward and it seemed very long. Finally he stood and bent over the bed and tucked her in briskly, reassuringly. But before he could straighten up and leave the room, she reached her arms around his neck and kissed him on the most prickly part of his day-old beard. Almost at once she pulled her blanket under her chin and closed her eyes. She didn't talk to herself as she had so many nights before, and the little smile curved the corner of her mouth as she settled down to sleep.

And it's really rather strange, but ever since that night, the little girl never again talked about wanting a horse.[4]

When we draw near to our children, when we let them know that we too are human, when we express our emotion in hugs and tears without fear of rejection, then our children will enjoy the greatest security they can ever know. They will understand that two people hover over them, love them dearly, and are willing to communicate their love at the deepest level of their lives.

I say it again: the only kind of love we can use is the love we feel.

Most of us will spend the rest of our lives learning how to love at that depth. But what a difference it makes at home!

9. Examine our own lives regularly.

What can we do to love our children and make them feel our love? If you miss everything else, please don't miss this. *We best communicate love for our children when they see that the commitment Mom and Dad have to each other is so deep they will never violate that commitment and leave the children to deal with the results.*

Many young people are growing up today in a totally fractured environment because Mom and Dad have been unwilling to examine their lives and their marriage before the Lord. They've been unwilling to extend the vigilance, put forth the effort, and pay the price to keep their marriage on a straight road and steady course. Listen, friend, if we can't muster the energy and courage to confront our marital strains out of love for one another, then at least let's make that effort out of concern for the welfare of our kids. Let's examine our own hearts regularly, and in the process grant our children a security they can ill afford to lose.

> "In the hassled, harried world in which we live, parents, it is easy to focus on the mess instead of the gift ... to miss the beauty of a hidden talent."
>
> —Chuck Swindoll

10. Exercise great patience with them.

It takes a lot of patience to be a parent. In fact, if it is true that "tribulation worketh patience," then parenting has got to be one of God's greatest tools to teach patience, because parenting and tribulation go together!

I've come to appreciate how God uses the hard experiences of life to enable us to love our children in a way we otherwise couldn't. My relationship with all of my children has been strengthened because of the difficult things we've experienced together.

As I look back, I see what God was doing and how He's used hard times to bind us together as a family and to awaken me out of a stupefying sleep over some things I should have known but didn't.

Thank God, the Lord is patient with me. So how can I do less than work at being patient with my own children?

Who would have thought?

Hidden away at the end of the little Old Testament book of Ruth is the announcement of a birth that would change the world:

> So Boaz took Ruth and she became his wife; and when
> he went in to her, the LORD gave her conception, and
> she bore a son....And they called his name Obed. He is
> the father of Jesse, the father of David (Ruth 4:13, 17).

You can understand the significance of this personal history only if you read it like Hebrew–that is, backwards. Reading it forwards makes you a prophet. History is read backwards.

If we could look ahead two generations, we might gain a whole new perspective on the importance of that little one God has given us. That little one God has put in our hands may be (hard to believe!) the grandfather or grandmother of someone great further down the line.

Little baby Obed blessed a marriage, a mother, a mother-in-law, and men and women everywhere–and he continues to bless us even to this day. Through the line of Boaz and Obed and Jesse and David eventually came the Lord Jesus Christ, our Redeemer. And so even you and I are blessed by his life–beyond words and beyond measure.

All of us ought to look at our little ones and say, "God help me, even though sometimes it is really hard, to see the potential wrapped up in this tiny bundle. God, if this little one is supposed to be a preacher someday, I'm OK with that. Or a teacher. Or a scientist. Or a typist. I just want her to be Your person. God, protect him from the influences of evil. Cause her to grow up to love You, and at an early age, to know You in a personal way. God, thank You for this blessing."

When God gives you such a blessing, you become its steward. Ask God to help you put your arms around him or her. Not just parental arms, but grandparental arms too. And the arms of brothers and sisters and uncles and aunts and nephews. Use all those embraces to love that child and guide that child and give that child the best possible opportunity to know God and to love God, and ultimately to bless others.

Oh, how God desires that! When I think of all the children God has blessed His people with, I see great storehouses of treasure piled high to the heavens. God has given us this treasure to nurture and to love, and we have a long-term responsibility to all those children every step along the way, all the way through. God gave babies as a blessing!

And who knows? Perhaps that little one sleeping in her crib will someday grow up to be President of the United States. Perhaps that tiny little boy will one day bring hope and encouragement to an entire generation by becoming a mighty preacher of God's amazing grace. Who knows?

If God has entrusted a little one to you, you are blessed. You have been given a reward. God has given you a heritage. Children are blessings from God.

And they are our future. We are to invest in them everything we are and everything we have, and they will carry into future generations all we are. Some day you will stand by your children when they find someone who loves the Lord, and with encouragement, strength and hope, you will watch them walk into the next phase of their lives together.

By the grace of God, you will have properly managed your home improvement loan. And the blessings will continue to roll on.

---

1 David Ferguson, *The Great Commandment Principle* (Wheaton, Ill.: Tyndale House Publishers, 1998), 203–204.

2 Dr. Joyce Brothers, "The Power of Love," *Good Housekeeping*, Sept. 1985, 103.

3 David Jeremiah, *Exposing the Myths of Parenthood* (Dallas:Word Publishing, 1988), 184.

4 Adapted from Barr Brown, "A Certain Man, a Little Girl, and a Horse," *Christian Century*, 3–10 June 1981, 643. Used by permission.

three

Building on a Solid Foundation

"Through wisdom is a house built,

And by understanding it is established;

By knowledge the rooms are filled

With all precious and pleasant riches."

—PROVERBS 24:3-4

*t*he family is God's idea.

If you go by its place in the Word of God, the family is one of God's first great ideas for us in this universe. In the very beginning of the Bible, God looks at the solitary man He has created and declares, "It is not good that man should be alone." So He brought a woman to the man, and the family began.

If God created the family, then doesn't it make sense that He might have something to say about how we could make it work? How it *should* work? God offers us some powerful truths to help us build families that will bring honor and glory to His name.

God's Word: The first foundation stone

There really is no other book in the history of the world quite like the Bible. It was written over a period of some 1,600 years, by all sorts of men, including fishermen, kings, shepherds, and philosophers. Yet all of their writings dovetail with each other. The Bible really is a miraculous book—and we could not ask for a better manual to help us build strong homes.

To get some idea of how amazing this book is, imagine that forty different physicians and surgeons, from seven different countries, speaking many languages, and writing over a period of 1,600 years, were to bring forth a medical textbook. Then think of taking these writings, most created independently of each other, and using them as the guide to treat some exotic disease.

What a mess *that* would be! Jumbled together would be the superstitions of sixteen centuries, magical incantations, all the foolishness of ancient days of darkness, together with the discoveries and inventions of modern science. Would you want such a book to govern the procedure for treatment of disease in our hospitals and doctor's offices? Would you want a surgeon following that manual to remove your appendix?

I don't think so.

If that's the way we operated today in the health care industry, I would find some other way to get better!

The illustration points out the real contrast between the Bible and all other books. It is indeed a miracle. There isn't anything else like it (or even close). This book comes to us from heaven–and that's why we can trust its advice for building solid homes on earth.

I believe this miracle nature of the Bible filled Paul's mind when he gave young Timothy a prescription for the perilous season of the last times. "All Scripture is God-breathed and is useful for teaching, rebuking, correcting and training in righteousness, so that the man of God may be thoroughly equipped for every good work" he writes in 2 Timothy 3:16-17 (NIV).

The apostle is telling Timothy there is one thing upon which he can count, one thing upon which he can build a solid foundation: the Word of God. We live in uncertain, confusing times, and when you live in a day when every wind of doctrine is blowing, you need to go back to the foundational truths found in the unchanging Word of God. Only there can we find the materials that will enable us to build strong homes.

Consider the single verse of 2 Timothy 3:16. A world of theology, a whole course of instruction, is given in that single verse. It is the crucial doctrine of all doctrines, because if it isn't true, the rest of our faith is nothing more than foolishness.

When the Bible says that all Scripture is inspired of God, it means that all Scripture is "breathed out" from God. Theologians would put it this way: God the Holy Spirit breathed out the Scripture into the lives and personalities of the individual writers, so that without denying their personality, they put down on paper the exact words that God would communicate to you and me if He were to speak audibly to us today.

We have in the Bible the written Word of God. It is not some human philosophy, not some individual's idea of how men ought to live, but a message from heaven with the stamp of Almighty God upon it. God's instructions come down to us in the pages of this book; this is what He has to say to you and to me. God breathed His words into the lives of men who, according to 2 Peter 1:21, were borne along by the Holy Spirit so that they wrote down exactly what God wanted us to know. The Bible is inspired throughout all its sixty-six books and is inspired to the extent even of its individual words.

And what is it good for? How can it profit us, especially in our roles as parents? That question in itself deserves a book, but for now let's concentrate merely on the four benefits Paul mentions to Timothy in 2 Timothy 3:16. As you read the following four benefits Paul lists, ask yourself, "Could I use any of these things in my home?" I think the answer will be clear.

Teaching-sound instruction, good for taking sure, safe, forward steps;

Rebuking-to bring conviction, which helps the erring one realize he or she is going the wrong way;

Correcting-heads us in the right direction, back to fellowship with God and others;

Training in righteousness-directs us to fuller, sweeter fellowship with others and with God.

Could your home use any of those things? Could you or your children benefit by seeing any of those four products of Scripture applied to your household? I don't really have to ask, do I?

And yet we haven't even begun to consider what happens in someone's life when he or she determines to live by the Scriptures. Paul says such a person will be "thoroughly equipped for every good work" (2 Timothy 3:17).

In the original language, the word translated "thoroughly equipped" means to be fitted like a socket into a joint; everything works smoothly. Such a person understands how she fits into the situation God put her in. He's not always anxiety-filled because he doesn't know why he's doing this or that. The person of God filled with the Word of God understands how he or she fits into the plan of God.

But not only that. Not only does he fit into his situation, he is *fitted* for his situation. Think of a seagoing vessel about to head into the ocean. In dry dock, workers are fitting this vessel for its voyage. They're stocking the shelves with food and are making sure the crew will have all the provisions they'll need at sea. They spend weeks and sometimes months loading that vessel with everything it could possibly require once it leaves dock.

That's the picture Paul paints for Timothy. He is saying, "Timothy, you're about to set sail on a sea of good works. And let me tell you how to get ready so you're fitted for every good work. You stock up the vessel of your soul with the Word of God; fill every shelf with the doctrine of God's Word. When you do that, you will find that you will be thoroughly equipped for every good work."

> "By reading the holy Scriptures, we are given a 'window' into the mind of the Father. What an incredible resource! The Creator who began with nothing-ness and made beautiful mountains and streams and clouds and cuddly little babies has elected to give us the inside story of the family. Marriage and parenthood were His ideas, and He tells us in His Word how to live together in peace and harmony."
>
> **—Dr. James Dobson**

Get the Bible in your heart and mind and into the hearts and minds of your children, and when you do, you'll find that when your family ship sets sail, you'll be ready for whatever storms you may face.

Back in 1742, John Albert Bengel observed that Scripture is the foundation of the church, and the church is the guardian of Scripture. When the church is healthy, the light of Scripture shines bright. When the church is sick, Scripture is corroded by neglect. And thus it happens that the outward form of Scripture and that of the church usually seem to exhibit, simultaneously, either health or sickness. And as a rule, the way in which the Scripture is being treated is in exact correspondence with the condition of the church.[1]

Spiritual health is linked inseparably to the Word of God. The great Old Testament renewal of Nehemiah's day began when all the people gathered themselves as one man into the street before the water gate and spoke to Ezra the scribe, asking him to bring out and explain to them the law of Moses.

Only as this Book takes center stage in the lives of God's people can we expect our families to thrive. One man wrote, "Let us remember that all the mischief, all the corruption and confusion, all the shame and dishonor, all the reproach and blas-phemy, had its origin in the neglect of the Word of God. It has ever been the special design of Satan to lead God's people away from Scripture. He will use anything and everything for this end. Tradition, the church, so-called expediency, human reason, popu-lar opinion, reputation and influence, character, position-all those he will use in order to get the heart and conscience away from the one golden sentence, that divine motto, 'It is written.'"[2]

From the Word of God we can glean principles to build our homes solidly and safely. The principles of the Word of God *work* in the home. Of course, the Bible is never read and taught merely so we can know more about it. It is always read and taught as a motivation to get going and do something about what we have heard. That's one of the things I love about the Bible. It tells us exactly what God wants of us, makes us totally responsible for it, then tells us what will happen if we do it and what will happen if we don't. That's the way it ought to be in our homes.

I am with those who sing the praises of God's Holy Book, the Bible. And with the hymn writer who has written these words that well express my gratitude to the Lord:

> Thank God for the Bible, whose clear, shining ray
> has lightened our path and turned night into day.
> Its wonderful treasures have never been told,
> more precious than riches set round with pure gold.
> Thank God for the Bible! In sickness and health
> it brings richer comfort than honors or wealth.
> Its blessings are boundless, an infinite store
> we may drink at the fountain and thirst nevermore.
> Thank God for the Bible! How dark is the night
> where no ray from its pages sheds forth its pure light.[3]

Some people say our culture has changed and that the principles of the Bible don't work in a modern world. But they are wrong. Scripture contains the best principles anywhere on Planet Earth. The principles of the Word of God are *timeless.* They are not culturally derived. They come from God and are just as relevant today as when they were written thousands of years ago. As we seek to build strong homes, we must not forget that before we can do anything else, we must get back to the Book.

The first step

> Unless the LORD builds the house,
> They labor in vain who build it
> (Psalm 127:1).

This psalm expresses the single most important scriptural truth in erecting a solid home: God must remain at the center. God has a wise plan for building strong homes, and unless we allow Him to build ours, they cannot stand. Psalm 127:1 insists that if we're to be successful, we must place God at the head of our home.

> "If we hope to do more than fantasize about family life, we need to sink our teeth into stuff that will stick to our ribs. . . . Our greatest need is fresh insight from our ever-relevant Lord whose Word is still unsurpassed as a source document of reliable counsel in any generation."
>
> —**Chuck Swindoll**

There is only one builder in the home: God. And there is only one architect for the home: God. God, who invented the home, wants to be at the head of the home. Until we put God at the center, all our attempts to make family life what we want it to be will end in frustration–no matter how worthy our motives! Unless we let Him build our homes, we will labor and strive and knock ourselves out to get down the road, only to think, *Is this it?*

Have you ever met people who thought that, if they could just get all the things they wanted, their family would be good, strong, and together? I have. Yet how many kids do you know who have all these things, but no family–so they hang out at your place? That's not God's plan. God has said He wants to be the head of our home.

I knew growing up that God was central in our home, but my conviction had little to do with the religious duties and rites you might expect. I didn't know God was at the head of my home because we read the Bible after dinner at night (even though we did). It wasn't that my parents were deeply involved in institutional ministry (although they were). Somehow, through all the stuff we did and all the activities we were involved in, God always occupied a big part of the picture–most of the time, the centerpiece. But wherever He was, He remained an integral part of our family. I couldn't escape it. Pervading our family life was the sense that God was supremely important.

A positive word of instruction

You might be surprised to learn that most of the information in the Word of God about child discipline is positive, not negative.

Discipline is training up our children in the way they should go, structuring their lives in a positive way so they will live according to the precepts we have set before them. Positive discipline is the focal point of the Book of Proverbs.

Consider Proverbs 22:6, for instance. Whenever we talk about parenting, that text immediately comes to mind. It says: "Train up a child in the way he should go, and when he is old he will not depart from it."

Some parents believe this verse promises that if we do what we're supposed to, we have a locked-in, absolute, trouble-free guarantee that while our children may have some ripples here, out there they'll be OK over the long haul. Now, I must confess I have never taken a great deal of comfort from that understanding. Who wants to be validated as a parent when you're too old to enjoy it?

Think about it. You let your kids sow their wild oats and plow through all their troubled times, and just when you're about to breathe your last and sink into the coffin, somebody tells you your kids are doing OK. Great. You've got about ten minutes to enjoy their good spiritual health before the undertaker shovels dirt over your face.

I don't know about you, but I want something more than that!

In fact, this famous passage does not carry a foolproof guarantee at all. No verse in the Book of Proverbs does. Proverbs isn't the book of promises; it's the book of proverbs, and that's quite a different thing.

The Book of Proverbs is a part of the "wisdom literature" of the Old Testament, written by the wisest man who ever lived. It is a list or a journal, if you will, of his observations about life.

In Proverbs 22:6, Solomon is simply saying that good parents normally rear good children. Parents who train their children in a godly way usually rear children who grow up into positive, responsible adults.

In his book *Parents in Pain*, Christian psychologist John White has this to say about Proverbs 22:6:

> If you examine its context, you will discover that the verse is not a promise made by God to anybody. It is a statement, a general statement about how family relationships normally work. It tells us what we can see

around us if we only open our eyes. Good parents usually produce good children; but when we interpret it as inflexible law, we are reading into it something the Holy Spirit never intended.[4]

So what did the Holy Spirit intend to convey through this verse? His instruction carries two main parts: (1) what is involved in *training up*; (2) what is involved in *the child's own way*.

1. What's involved in "training up"?

What does it mean to "train up"? The term is used in the Old Testament just three other times, in all three instances to convey the idea of dedication–once to describe the dedication of Solomon's house, twice to convey the idea of dedicating the temple. The word originally related to the palate of the mouth. An Arab midwife would rub crushed dates on the palate of a baby's mouth to create the instinctive action to suck, so that the child could be nourished. Over time the concept of training up came to mean "to create a thirst or a hunger within a child for the godly things of life."

Sometimes we've given the concept a military flavor. "Get in shape!" "I'm training you up, boy!" But it's not like that at all. This isn't boot camp; it has to do with creating within the child a thirst and a hunger for the things of God.

2. What's involved in "the child's own way"?

The Scripture says we create a thirst and a hunger for the things of God by training a child up "in the way he should go"–or more literally, "according to his own way."

That's a telling phrase. Once and for all it does away with the comparative analysis that goes on in some Christian families: "Johnny, why aren't you like your brother Gene?" Well, there's one simple reason: he's *not* like his brother Gene because he's not his brother Gene! He is himself. Unique. An individual.

This text says that as parents, we're to study the individual characteristics of each of our children. And then, as we come to understand how they "tick," we're to create in them this thirst for God. One family counselor I read said, "It would be a wise thing if parents made a note-book on every one of their children and then made observations in that notebook as they begin to understand what makes that child tick, why they are the way they are. And you know, children in one family are *diversely* different."

My daughter Jennifer used to baffle me when she was a little girl. When she did something really bad and got a spanking, she refused to cry. You couldn't make her cry. Her stoic self-composure overwhelmed me. But as soon as you stopped spanking her and put your arms around her and told her that you loved her, Niagara Falls spilled over. She was the only one of our children who ever responded that way.

Children are different, aren't they? You can't train up one child the way you train up another. Proverbs 22:6 tells us to create within our child a thirst for God according to the way he or she should go–and if we do that, the probability is great that he or she will embrace the very things of God we embrace. We will have given him or her the best possible chance to grow into spiritual maturity.

Protect your family from destructive influences

God is the only builder and architect of our homes. But He uses at least two laborers to do much of the work: Mom and Dad. We work together with Him on the same project, not only to build, but to protect.

Psalm 127:1 not only says, "Unless the LORD builds the house, they labor in vain who build it," it concludes, "Unless the LORD guards the city, the watchman stays awake in vain."

There is One who builds, and we build with Him.

There is One who watches, and we watch with Him.

We're in partnership with God in *building* our homes as well as in *protecting* our homes.

And how can we protect our homes? One of the most important ways we fulfill this critical duty is to pray for them. And that introduces the second foundation stone of a well-built Christian home.

Prayer: The second foundation stone

A wonderful Christian family owned a parrot whose vocabulary consisted of a solitary phrase: "Let's kiss." Every time somebody visited that family, the parrot began speaking the only phrase it knew, which embarrassed the family no end.

One day some members of this family were talking with some friends who also owned a parrot. Soon they got to sharing parrot stories and the friends said, "We have a parrot too. And it knows only one phrase: 'Let's pray.'"

The first family thought it would be wonderful to have a parrot with a spiritual vocabulary. They hoped that if they put their parrot with their friends' parrot, their bird might learn how to say, "Let's pray." So they arranged for the two parrots to meet. They put their parrot in the cage with the spiritual parrot and watched to see what would happen. Sure enough, the unspiritual parrot hadn't been in the cage for five seconds before it said, "Let's kiss."

And the spiritual parrot replied, "Glory! My prayers have been answered."

Prayer really works

I can't vouch for the truth of this story, but I can vouch for the power of prayer. The Bible insists that God hears and answers believing prayer. And it further declares that prayer changes things, even in our homes. Consider just a little of the Bible's teaching on prayer:

> Call to Me, and I will answer you, and show you great and mighty things, which you do not know (Jeremiah 33:3).

> So I say to you, ask, and it will be given to you; seek, and you will find; knock, and it will be opened to you. For everyone who asks receives and he who seeks finds, and to him who knocks it will be opened (Luke 11:9-10).

> If you ask anything in My name, I will do it (John 14:14).

> Whatever you ask in prayer, believing, you will receive (Matthew 21:22).

> If you abide in Me, and My words abide in you, you will ask what you desire, and it shall be done for you (John 15:7).

The effective, fervent prayer of a righteous man avails much (James 5:16).

Those promises from the Word of God tell us, simply, that *prayer works.* If you pray, God will hear you, and He will leap into action on your behalf, just as He did for believers in Bible times:

- God is able to save three of His followers from a fiery furnace (Daniel 3:17).
- God is able to save Daniel from the lions' mouths (Daniel 6:20-22).
- God is able to give a child to a ninety-year-old Sarah (Romans 4:18-22).
- God is able to give His followers all they need (2 Corinthians 9:8).
- God is able to save completely those who come to God through Jesus Christ (Hebrews 7:25).
- God is able to do immeasurably more than we can ask or imagine (Ephesians 3:20).

God is able!

If you believe this and don't pray, something's not tracking in the way you think. Perhaps you don't know God as well as you suppose. As one author wrote:

There is a direct correlation between not knowing Jesus well and not asking much from him. A failure in our prayer life is generally a failure to know Jesus. A prayer-less Christian is like a bus driver trying alone to push his bus out of a rut because he doesn't know Clark Kent is on board. A prayerless Christian is like having your room wallpapered with Sak's Fifth Avenue gift certificates but always shopping at Ragstock because you can't read. "If you knew the gift of God and who it is that speaks to you, [says Jesus to the woman at the well in John 4] you would ask-*you would ask!*" And the implication is that those who do ask–Christians who spend time in prayer–do it because they see that God is a great Giver and that Christ is wise and merciful and powerful beyond measure.[6]

Several years ago Bill Hybels wrote a book titled *Too Busy Not to Pray.* In it, he makes this statement:

> *"Family worship should include a time when you talk to God. Early in our family life, we used a loose-leaf notebook. On one side was written, 'We ask,' and on the other side, 'He answers.' I wouldn't exchange for anything what this taught my children about the theology of prayer."*
>
> **—Howard Hendricks**

When I began praying in earnest, I discovered this...if you are willing to invite God to involve himself in your daily challenges, you will experience his prevailing power–in your home, in your relationships, in the marketplace, in the schools, in the church, wherever it is most needed.

The other side of that equation is sobering: it is hard for God to release his power in your life when you put your hands in your pockets and say, "I can handle it on my own." If you do that, don't be surprised if one day you get the nagging feeling that the tide of battle has shifted against you and that you're fairly powerless to do anything about it.

Prayerless people cut themselves off from God's prevailing power and the frequent result is the familiar feeling of being overwhelmed, overrun, beaten down, pushed around, defeated. Surprising numbers of people are willing to settle for lives like that. Don't be one of them. Nobody has to live like that. Prayer is the key to unlocking God's prevailing power in your life.[7]

Oh, if we could only get our hearts in tune with this truth! God is able! He hears and answers prayer! And He invites busy moms and dads to come to Him every day, to lay their problems and challenges at His feet, and watch Him work. *Prayer really works!*

Secular confirmation

In *Healing Words: The Power of Prayer and the Practice of Medicine*, Larry Dossey tells how astonished he was to find over fifty published studies–all using good science–that showed prayer brings about significant changes in the ones prayed for. Dossey is no fundamentalist, but he was so convinced of the evidence that he declared physicians who don't pray for their patients are guilty of malpractice. He insists that science confirms the healing power of prayer.

"Experiments with people showed that prayer positively affected high blood pressure, wounds, heart attacks, headaches and anxiety..." Dossey wrote. And these effects did not depend on whether the person prayed for was present or far away; healing took place either on-site or at a distance. Nothing seemed capable of stopping or blocking prayer.[8]

In 1988 Randolph Byrd, M.D., carried out one of the most significant studies on prayer. In a carefully controlled experiment, 393 patients in the coronary unit at San Francisco General Hospital were randomly divided into two groups. Half the group received intercessory prayer from devout Christians who had an "active Christian life as manifested by daily devotional prayer and active Christian fellowship with a local church." Each patient's name and general condition was given to the prayer groups who agreed to pray for his or her recovery. The other patients served as the control group.

When all the differences were submitted to a multivariant analysis, those who received prayer fared significantly better than those who had not. Only two explanations exist for the improved status of the prayer group: (1) the change occurred due to chance; (2) the change occurred as the result of prayer. The odds of improved health due to chance were one in 10,000. So unless you think the patients involved in this study just happened to hit that one in 10,000, the difference can safely be attributed to prayer.

The writer concluded, "Had this been the evaluation of a new drug designed to improve the overall status of patients in coronary care units, it would have been heralded as a breakthrough and rushed into service."[9]

Secular studies confirm what the Bible has always maintained: prayer works! Remember, these are not evangelical studies. They aren't guesses or hopes or estimations. These are scientific studies that confirm the efficacy of prayer.

And prayer works in the home just as surely as it works in the hospital!

One reason why Christians generally enjoy healthier lives than others is that they are always growing in their ability to pray–and not only that, they have a whole cadre of people around them who pray for them. There are more people praying for me all over the world than I knew existed. It is incredible to *feel* the power of prayer. I'm no mystic, but I want to testify that I feel the power of prayer in my life.

I am so very thankful that I am a Christ-follower! Not only do I have eternity settled, not only do I know that Jesus Christ lives in my heart, not only do I have the Holy Spirit filling me every day–but I am indescribably thankful for all the wonderful blessings that are mine through the abundant life God has given me. And God offers that same life to you and your family, through prayer.

What shall we pray about?

If it's true that prayer changes things, what sorts of issues can we pray about regarding our families? How should we pray for our spouse and children? What petitions can we bring to God's attention?

Author Patrick Morley offered a list of concerns we parents can pray for regarding our kids:

- pray for a saving faith if they don't know the Lord;
- pray for a growing faith if they're immature;
- pray for an independent faith as they get older;
- pray that they will be strong and healthy in mind and body and spirit;
- pray for a sense of purpose and destiny in their life;
- pray for a desire within them that they will have integrity; for a call to excellence;
- pray that they would understand the ministry God has for them;

- pray that they will set aside times to spend with God;
- pray that they will acquire wisdom;
- pray for protection against drugs and alcohol and premarital sex.[10]

If I had to reduce it to just one thing, I would appeal to the story of Mary and Martha in Luke 10:41-42 where Jesus said, "Martha, Martha, you are worried and troubled about many things. But one thing is needed." He was talking about her personal relationship with the Lord Jesus. If your children's personal relationships with Jesus are solid, most of the other stuff will settle in. So I pray about my kids' walk with God and their faithfulness to the Lord.

Never has there been a time when we need to pray for our kids more than today. They're fighting battles we can't imagine. They need to know that Mom and Dad are standing with them and praying for them.

Some years ago Donna and I made this a priority. Sometimes we struggled with praying together for the important things. Our praying wasn't always as focused as we wanted it to be. But parents get focused real quick when a bunch of teenagers live in their home. Boy, do you suddenly sense the need for prayer! So we devised a prayer plan. We decided to combine early-morning walking and praying and we continue the practice even today.

We stumble out of bed and don't say much for the first few steps. About half way around, I begin to pray. Sometimes I start at the lower end of the family and sometimes I start at the top. I'll just say, "Lord, today be good to Jan." I pray for her and for everything that's happening in her life. When I'm finished, I stop and Donna picks it up and prays for David. When she's finished, I begin praying for Jennifer. And when I'm through, Donna wraps it up and prays for Daniel. So we pray through our four children.

We usually don't pray for the same child each day, but as a couple we pray for them all. We bring them to the Lord and ask God to care for them.

It's an incredible time of oneness together and it's critical for us because we're the only two laborers building this house. God's the builder and the architect, but we're the laborers. It's a bonding time for us and it's thrilling to see how God answers our prayers.

It's also a wonderful time of communication. When I hear their mother pray, I learn a lot about our kids that I didn't know before. A couple of times we've been walking along the street and I've said, "*What was that?*"

Some days I have felt so burdened for my family that I have spent my whole prayer time praying for my children, either out loud or in writing, making sure I said everything I wanted to say. And God has answered my prayers in a way that would take ten books to describe.

I keep pictures of all four of our children and of our grandchild in my prayer journal. In that prayer journal I list their special needs. And as I pray for those needs, at the throne of grace I feel a sense of closeness to my loved ones who may be so far away. Through prayer I was able to touch my son when he lived three thousand miles away. I talked to him on the phone, but I also stayed in touch with him through prayer as I brought him to God every day. I couldn't determine what was going to happen in David and Cami's life, but I could talk to God about it, and God heard. He knew where Raleigh, North Carolina was.

Perhaps your children are (or will be) scattered around the country or the world. Remember this: prayer brings Cedarville, Ohio, and San Diego, California, together before the throne of grace. Prayer brings Toronto, Canada, together with Kansas City, Missouri, and at the throne of grace we meet and there bring the needs of our children to our Heavenly Father. And somehow, though we are separated by hundreds of miles, we feel a sense of oneness in the presence of our God, a sense of security that God will do what He's promised.

Your children may still live with or near you, but through prayer you can draw even closer to them than physical proximity allows. In prayer your soul can reach out to them in the deepest part of their being, and at the throne of grace your spirit can touch their spirit as you both breathe in the pure, holy air of heaven. If I were you, I'd take in as many lungfuls as I could.

Praying for their mates

Not only do we enjoy the privilege of praying about the current challenges our children face, we also can begin praying for events still far down the track. As we look out on the cultural carnage today and realize how much tragedy exists even in Christian homes, we would be wise to begin praying for our children's mates, long before they're ready to get married.

Years ago I visited a friend who at the time pastored a church in Kansas City, Missouri. I was staying in his home and joined his wife and teenagers for family devotions. As he began to pray, I was awestruck that he began to pray for each of his kids like this: "O God, keep [then he would mention his daughter's name] from divorce." Then he would pray for the next one, "O God, keep him from divorce." And I remember thinking, *I must be missing something here.*

After the prayer session ended and the children went to bed, I asked my friend, "Wasn't that a rather strange way to pray for your unmarried children?" He said, "Oh, not at all. Through my counseling I have discovered that most divorces begin before marriage ever starts. And so I pray for my children that they will be spared from divorce, because I realize that the most critical part of that prayer will be answered the day they stand before an altar and say 'I do.' If they have not carefully and prayerfully chosen that person with whom they will spend the rest of their lives, they are likely to add to the nation's high divorce statistics."

Parents, years before the weddings are planned, we need to pray for our children in their choice of a life partner. Those prayers need to begin *long* before any one particular candidate comes into view. Quite often, once that person has been chosen, it is too late to begin praying. We need to pray that God will help our children as they date and get exposed to "marital possibilities." We need to plead with God to give them wisdom to sort out the process that will ultimately lead to marriage.

This is profoundly biblical, you know. Way back in Genesis 24 we read that when Abraham sent his chief servant to find a godly wife for Isaac, the servant began his search by praying to God for guidance and instruction. So we learn in the very first book of the Bible that picking a marriage partner is a matter of prayer. This man, seeking for a wife in proxy for his master, understood his task to be so awesome that he needed to bathe it in prayer.

Outside of choosing to commit their lives to Jesus Christ, picking a marriage partner is the most critical decision our children will ever make, a decision that will affect the rest of their lives. Surely, then, it is an unspeakable privilege to add this item to our regular prayer ministry!

Prayer: The greatest thing you can do

Have you ever heard empty-nester parents say something like, "Well, they're all gone now. All I can do is pray"?

All you can do?

Sometimes it sounds as if all the real work is done, all the effective labor accomplished, with prayer the only feeble resource left.

I used to think that prayer for little ones was more important than for grown-up kids, because, after all, youngsters can run away, get lost in the mall, or otherwise go missing. When they're little, we parents enjoy a real sense of control. We sense we can do something concrete for our kids: build fences around the yard, make sure we tightly hold onto their hands in crowds, give them rides to school. But the older they get-the more they sprout wings, the more independent they become, the more they begin to live their own lives-the more we sense we have lost influence and control...and the only thing left to do is to pray for them.

I want to shout that the *only* thing we can do is the *greatest* thing we can do.

"The prayer of a righteous man is powerful and effective," says the Book of James (5:16, NIV). "The king's heart is in the hand of the LORD, like the rivers of water; He turns it wherever He wishes," says Proverbs (21:1).

"It is impossible for me to overstate the need for prayer in the fabric of family life. Being able to bow in prayer as the day begins or ends gives expression to the frustrations and concerns that might not otherwise be ventilated. On the other end of that prayer line is a loving heavenly Father who has promised to hear and answer our petitions. In this day of disintegrating families on every side, we dare not try to make it on our own."

—Dr. James Dobson

So what happens when a righteous man prays that the heart of a king might be turned? Ask Nehemiah. In his case, whole cities were repopulated, ruined walls were rebuilt, and the worship of the one true God was restored to a entire battered nation (Nehemiah 2:4-5).

Listen: what's true of kings is equally true of spouses and sons and daughters. Through prayer, righteous parents can change the course and direction of their family. The prayer of a righteous parent can put a child's heart in the hand of the Lord, who then directs it like a watercourse wherever He pleases.

So let's pray!

A place to call home

"Through wisdom a house is built, and by understanding it is established; by knowledge the rooms are filled with all precious and pleasant riches," says Proverbs 24:3-4. If we are to be wise parents, we will gladly acknowledge God as the builder and architect of our homes. We will joyfully give Him first place under our roofs and will labor to build our homes on the unshakable foundation stones of God's Word and believing prayer.

When we do that, the Bible tells us we can expect nothing less than a house "filled with all precious and pleasant riches." That's a place worth living in! And it's a place our kids will be delighted to call home.

---

1 John Albert Bengel, *New Testament Word Studies*, translator: Charlton T. Lewis et. al., (Grand Rapids: Kregel Publications, 1971), xiii.

2 Author unknown.

3 "Thank God for the Bible," *The Voice of Thanksgiving Hymnal*, (Chicago: Moody Press, 1928), 4.

4 John White, *Parents in Pain* (Downers Grove, Ill.: InterVarsity Press, 1979), 43.

5 Author unknown.

6 John Piper, *Desiring God*, tenth anniversary expanded edition (Sisters, Ore.: Multnomah Books, 1996), 139.

7 Bill Hybels, *Too Busy Not to Pray* (Downers Grove, Ill.: InterVarsity Press, 1988), 13.

8 Larry Dossey, M.D., *Healing Words: The Power of Prayer and the Practice of Medicine*, 1993, Harper, San Francisco.

9 Dr. Randolph Byrd, "Positive therapeutic effects of intercessory prayer in a coronary unit population," *Southern Medical Journal*, July, 1988; 81(7): 826–29.

10 Adapted from Patrick M. Morley, *The Man in the Mirror* (Nashville: Thomas Nelson Publishers, 1992), 97.

Four

The Benefits of a
Christian Home

"Affirming words from moms and dads

are like light switches. Speak a word of affirmation

at the right moment in a child's life

and it's like lighting up a whole roomful of possibilities."

—GARY SMALLEY AND JOHN TRENT

*t*he Christian family is not only alive and well, it is flourishing.

Social scientists have put it under their collective microscopes-and have been astounded at what they are finding. Significantly, these are not Christians studying the families of fellow believers; these are committed secularists finding out the truth through impartial scientific processes.

Marianne K. Hering reported some of these findings in a *Focus on the Family* article titled "Believe Well, Live Well." The article began like this:

> Pluck any man out of a church pew on Sunday morning and liken him to a neighbor who's still at home, pouring through the two-pound Sunday newspaper in his easy chair. Let's say the two are of the same age and earn comparable salaries. Neither of them smokes, drinks or plays the lottery. Both floss their teeth, collect baseball cards and enjoy cheesecake.
>
> Which man will live longer and enjoy the benefits of a stable marriage? Answer: the man (or woman) in the pew. In recent years, scientific research is backing up what common sense has told us for years, mainly that churchgoers live longer, stay married and feel happier than those who say they don't believe in God.[1]

In the last few years, the message of this article (and many others like it) have overwhelmed me with their remarkable conclusions. Some of their findings almost jumped off the pages and into my heart. Substantial secular evidence now confirms many of the things we Christians have believed and attempted to practice all of our lives.

In this chapter I would like to focus on some of those findings. And the question we want to answer is this: Does living out our Christian faith make a positive difference in our lives away from church? Or put another way: What benefits to our family might we expect to reap when we take Christianity seriously?

This chapter could be a lot longer than it is-the news is *that* good-but for our purposes let's focus on three areas in which the studies have confirmed what the Bible has told us all along.

Christians live longer and healthier lives

Psalm 128 gives us good biblical warrant to believe that a healthy faith leads to a healthy home life. The psalm says:

> Blessed is every one who fears the LORD,
> Who walks in His ways....
> The LORD bless you out of Zion,
> And may you see the good of Jerusalem
> All the days of your life.
> Yes, may you see your children's children.
> Peace be upon Israel!
> (Psalm 128:1, 5-6)

The psalmist here proclaims that both health and long life attach to a vibrant, robust faith in the living God.

This length-of-days concept appears quite often in the Book of Proverbs. Proverbs 10:27 (NIV), for example, says, "The fear of the LORD adds length to life, but the years of the wicked are cut short."

Exodus 20:12 presents our children with a tantalizing proposition about their futures-it's the Law, if you will. That verse says, "Honor your father and your mother, that your days may be long upon the land which the LORD your God is giving you."

The contention is repeated in Deuteronomy 5:16: "Honor your father and your mother, as the LORD your God has commanded you, that your days may be long, and that it may be well with you in the land which the LORD your God is giving you."

In New Testament times the Apostle Paul picked up on those statements and in Ephesians 6:2-3 observed that this Old Testament command to children is the first to carry a promise, namely, that those who follow the paths of godliness in their homes will live longer.

Pretty straightforward, isn't it? Honor God with your life, and God will honor you with a life that's longer. In a nutshell, that's the Bible's position on this topic. But what do the studies say? Do they have any evidence that would tend to confirm this promise from a scientific standpoint? Among other things, the studies revealed the following:

- People who practice their faith have less risk of heart disease.
- People who practice their faith have lower blood pressure.
- People who practice their faith spend less time in the hospital.[2]

Of course, this isn't a guarantee that godliness always and invariably leads to sound health. I know that all too well. Some time ago cancer invaded my life and during my struggle, people from all over the world sent me books suggesting how to deal with my disease. I have a drawer in my office full of such volumes. Had I attempted to read them all, I wouldn't have gotten anything else done. But I find it incredible that in almost every book I have read–even books by authors blatantly opposed to a personal relationship with God through Jesus Christ–all talk about the importance of prayer and a "spiritual center." Many authors don't know what such a spiritual center might be, but they're certain that people who enjoy a personal relationship with God have found something powerfully healing.

One author said that religious people tend to live longer because they don't commit suicide as often as the nonreligious. (That would skew the statistics a bit!) A review in *Christianity Today* of literature delving into why people take their own lives concurred with this author; the article showed that a strong religious commitment provided the best protection against suicide. And the fear of God seems to function even for the severely depressed: "Religious patients realize that the first person they are going to meet after suicide is God. What a horrible way to introduce yourself!"[3]

> "The years fly by so quickly. Opportunities to drop seeds of affirmation into the soul of a child's heart may not be as numerous as we might imagine. Let's set aside some of our many 'important' distractions and make sure this great good gets done in our homes ... even today."
>
> **—Gary Smalley and John Trent**

A mountain of statistical information, growing every year, tells us that huge advantages belong to God-fearing, Christ-following believers. Studies by secular people using good science indicate that if you follow Christ and practice your faith, you are far more likely to live a longer, healthier life than someone who tries to live without God.

Christians are more successful in their professions
Is it really true that God has promised committed followers of Christ greater success in life? Could that be possible? A number of Scriptures certainly seem to promise exactly that.

Verses 2 and 4 of Psalm 128 (NIV) say, "You will eat the fruit of your labor; blessings and prosperity will be yours.... Thus is the man blessed who fears the LORD."

The same truth-that success in business accompanies and graces a godly lifestyle-is communicated in many places in Scripture. For example, consider Joshua 1:8:

> This Book of the Law shall not depart from your mouth, but you shall meditate in it day and night, that you may observe to do according to all that is written in it. For *then you will make your way prosperous, and then you will have good success* (italics added).

If you follow God by obeying His Word, this text seems to say you will enjoy a prosperous and successful life. How else could one read it?

And Joshua isn't alone in this contention. Next consider a passage from a very familiar portion of the Old Testament. Read it carefully, because although you may think you know it, the text may hold some surprises for you.

> Blessed is the man
> Who walks not in the counsel of the ungodly,
> Nor stands in the path of sinners,
> Nor sits in the seat of the scornful;
> But his delight is in the law of the LORD,
> And in His law he meditates day and night.

> He shall be like a tree
> Planted by the rivers of water,
> That brings forth its fruit in its season,
> Whose leaf also shall not wither;
> And whatever he does shall prosper
> (Psalm 1:1-3).

Isn't that interesting? A person who follows Christ, a man or woman who knows and obeys the Word of God, has a leg up on those who don't. If we commit ourselves to Jesus Christ, the Bible insists we have an opportunity to enjoy real success and prosperity.

One man in the Old Testament epitomized this. The patriarch Joseph is one of the great men of the Bible and a personal hero of mine. When his brothers sold young Joseph into Egyptian slavery and he became the servant of Potiphar, the text says this about him:

> Now Joseph had been taken down to Egypt. And Potiphar, an officer of Pharaoh, captain of the guard, an Egyptian, bought him from the Ishmaelites who had taken him down there. The LORD was with Joseph, *and he was a successful man;* and he was in the house of his master the Egyptian. And his master saw that the LORD was with him and that *the LORD made all he did to prosper in his hand* (Genesis 39:1-3, italics added).

Joseph was called a prosperous, successful man, even in the land of his captivity. Why? The Bible gives us the key: the Lord was with him.

If you need a business partner, let me recommend the Lord. If He is with you, if you walk with Him and follow the principles of His Holy Word, God has said He will bless you. He will never steal from you, deceive you, dishonor you, undervalue you, take the business away from you, or leave you with all the work. What a Partner!

Of course, this doesn't mean you won't suffer through down times. It doesn't mean you won't encounter unexpected bends in the road and disruptive moments (remember, after a short stint in Potiphar's house, this same Joseph was wrongfully accused of attempted rape and wound up in a stinking prison for at least two years). But it does mean that, looking across the face of God's earth at the landscape of human experience, those who follow Christ and who commit themselves to the principles of the Word of God will usually be more successful in their professional lives than those who do not.

Before we look at the studies that corroborate this encouraging idea, let me take a quick side trip to make sure we avoid an error that some have made in proclaiming this teaching. Allow me to do so by quoting author Florence Bulle:

> The deception in the success-prosperity doctrine is subtle. It sounds so spiritual to assert that we cannot be sick or fail if we trust God, and that He will reward us for faith and giving and being good, by making us rich in material things. But this was not the message of the early church fathers. Nor was it the message of the men and women of faith who throughout history set church and nation aflame with revival.
>
> The more we pursue such poppycock, the more likely we will end up like pampered children. Getting everything we want won't turn us into soldiers for Christ. We may wear a tailored suit with gold buttons and hash marks, but we will be no more soldiers than the six-year-old with his feet shoved into his dad's old combat boots and carrying a wooden gun. Unchecked, the prosperity-success syndrome will not see Christians developing together into a vigorous, stouthearted, indomitable church. Rather, it will reduce the body of Christ to spiritual flabbiness.[4]

God does promise in the Old Testament that prosperity usually accompanies godliness, but we must never forget that no room exists in godliness for greed or selfishness. True prosperity consists not simply in material gain, but also in spiritual growth-and few things help us grow more than giving away what we have, whether that be our resources, our faith, or our lives.

But back to the main point. Does a commitment to God, demonstrated by a growing, living faith, actually help to prosper a person's business? The studies answer with a resounding, "Yes!" Keep in mind these studies were not generated by Christian people trying to validate their faith, but were conducted by secular people interested only in what the numbers told them. When they put two and two together they came up with four, just like every other competent mathematician.

So what does the research show? Consider this:

> A survey conducted by Korn-Ferry International (a New York executive search firm) in conjunction with the UCLA School of Management revealed that in a group of 1,361 vice-presidents of major corporations, 89 percent of them were active in their faith. Eighty-seven percent were still married to their one and only spouse, and 92 percent were raised by two-parent families.[5]

"By cultivating what God has placed into our children's lives, we bring out those capabilities and we 'kiss' them into reality. Affectionately hovering over our brood, we hatch those eggs, and each child grows up trusting in God, yes, but also believing in himself . . . which causes him to think, I am valuable."

—Chuck Swindoll

This study suggests that the highly successful people it observed grew up in strong, two-parent families where faith was taken seriously-and now, even at their high level of achievement, they still practice the faith of their childhood. The study concluded, "It is difficult to divorce this part of their spiritual life from the success which seemed so evident in their professional life."

Zig Ziglar, noted motivational speaker and a godly layman who teaches a Sunday School class for a large Baptist church in Dallas, wrote in one of his books,

> The church is interwoven in every facet of our life. In the corporate world, those who have faith do better than those who do not. *Fortune Magazine* revealed that

> 91 percent of the CEOs of the "Fortune 500 Companies"
> claimed a church affiliation, indicating that to a degree
> their accomplishments were the result of the values
> they learned either in church or from the Bible. Since 54
> percent came from lower-middle class or poor families,
> the evidence is good that the church played a role in
> their accomplishments.[6]

The evidence is in, and it's good news for our side. When we live and raise our families in a godly environment, we're setting up our kids for success in later life. The Bible proclaims that fact and modern research confirms it.

Christians are better able to pass on their values

People with strong moral values normally want to pass on those values to their children, to perpetuate a godly influence in the next generation. They want to see their values continue. Certainly this is something Donna and I have attempted to do in our family. So how does one best do this?

Another look at Psalm 128 reveals a beautifully rendered picture of family unity. Verse 3 says, "Your wife shall be like a fruitful vine in the very heart of your house, your children like olive plants all around your table."

Here is a lovely picture of a family living together in harmony, committed in unity, one to another. The Bible says God blesses our children when we honor Him with our lives.

Of course there are exceptions, and some very godly parents could reply, "Dr. Jeremiah, we have lived for God all of our lives and we have done everything we know how to do, humanly speaking. Yet we have a child who has rebelled against it all. So how can your take on this verse be accurate?"

To such grieving parents I would say, first, that the final chapter in the life of your child isn't yet written. Unless that child has already died in a state of rebellion, God may still bring him or her around. It's happened before.

But second, this verse is like those from Proverbs; it's not a guaranteed formula that works 100 percent of the time. It too is an example of wisdom literature, and wisdom literature tells us how life normally turns out. Proverbial statements tell us that when we follow God's way, we can generally expect a positive outcome. Proverbial wisdom isn't a promise, but more like a statistical probability. In fact, that is exactly what the studies we're about to consider tell us. None of the percentages are 100, but they do insist that when we rear our children in a godly way, we normally can expect highly positive results.

"But what about a troubling passage that suggests just the reverse?" some have asked me over the years. "What about the verse in Exodus 20 that warns about the sins of the fathers being passed down through the generations? How do you respond to that?"

The anxious parents who pose this question have in mind the second half of Exodus 20:5, where God says, "I, the LORD your God, am a jealous God, visiting the iniquity of the fathers upon the children to the third and fourth generations of those who hate Me." They know of some father who really messed up his life, and noted with sadness that his children followed his destructive ways. And they insist, "You see, that's the way it is. The father messed up royally, then his son messed up royally, and his son probably will mess up royally too. You see what happens? Whenever you do something wrong in your family, you pay for it for two or three generations."

While I'm sure we are all the products of homes that in one way or another failed to live up to biblical standards, it bothers me that those who camp on "generational curses" never read the very next verse. If they did, they would not focus on the negative, but the positive. In Exodus 20:6 (NIV) God immediately says that He shows "love to thousands [of generations] who love me and keep my commandments."

Do you see the Lord's main point? He emphasizes not the divine judgment on four generations of men who hate Him, but the love He lavishes on the thousand generations who love Him. The theme is not decades of generational curses, but centuries of generational blessings!

This encouraging message is repeated for emphasis in Deuteronomy 7:9:

> Therefore know that the LORD your God, He is God,
> the faithful God who keeps covenant and mercy for a

thousand generations with those who love Him and keep His commandments.

A father's ungodly lifestyle may cause family heartaches for a few generations, but God Himself declares that a father's godliness can extend its blessed reach into a *thousand* generations. As Paul wrote, "Where sin abounded, grace abounded much more" (Romans 5:20).

When we love God with all our hearts, we can begin a generational continuity that may go on forever in the lives of those who follow us! The Bible says that we Christians can pass on our faith to our children, to our children's children, and to their children beyond them for countless scores of years, and that through them we can shake a world we will never see. That's the way faith works!

An article titled "Our Spiritual Family Tree," by Richard Thomas Bewes, illustrates this point:

> It was through a single sermon, preached last century by D.L. Moody, that the principle of generational continuity-transmitting a value system from family to family through the corridors of time-stamped itself indelibly upon the mindset of my own family in Britain.
>
> The year was 1882, and D.L. Moody, at forty-five years of age and at the height of his power, was in the middle of a whirlwind campaign through several major British cities....September 26 found the famed evangelist...in Plymouth. That evening my future grandfather, then fourteen-year-old Tommy Bewes, sat entranced-first with the singing of Ira D. Sankey and then with Moody's preaching.
>
> It seems that Tommy was the only family member who attended the meeting, unable to persuade any of the others to come along. We even know what text was preached that night because Tommy wrote a memorable letter to his sister Evy that has somehow survived to this day: "I am writing to tell you some good news which you will be glad to hear. I went to one of Moody's and

Sankey's meetings on Tuesday and there I was saved. He spoke from the 9th verse of the 3rd of Genesis. It is 'Where art thou?' He said that that was the first question that God ever asked man in the Bible and that it was the first question that people ought to ask themselves."

Then the writer of this article, the grandson of the fourteen-year-old Tommy who was saved in D.L. Moody's meeting so long ago, wrote:

One solitary sermon–and three generations later we are still feeling the effects of it. Before this event, my family had not been particularly noted for evangelical influence.... Today we are a large family with many evangelical connections. It was Moody's sermon that imparted the new impulse.

My grandfather went on to study for the Christian ministry at Cambridge University. His eldest son, Cecil, my father, did likewise. He spent more than twenty years building up the growing churches of Kenya in East Africa. Four of us grandchildren entered the ordained ministry; several others were to marry evangelical clergymen, still others were to be involved in the missions and councils of Christian enterprise and service...all because of one solitary sermon.... Our family story is nothing unusual...it is simply the principle of spiritual continuity in the family.[7]

Does this happen today? You bet it does. Those who don't know my history might think that I hail from a long line of preachers going back to my grandfather's days in Wales. That would be a mistaken assumption. I am but a second generation Christian; my father became the first believer in his family.

At nineteen years of age, my dad was invited to a basketball outreach at the First Baptist Church in Johnson City, New York. He went, not because he was seeking God, but because he was a good basketball player and wanted to play. Through that outreach, my father became a Christian and got so excited about the things of God he began attending the Baptist Bible Seminary in Johnson City in order to become a pastor. Later I was born, and today I'm a pastor.

I'm happy to report that just a short time before my grandfather died, he accepted Jesus Christ as his personal Savior-but he entered the kingdom long after my father came to faith. My dad was the first Christian in our family. I'm second generation, and my kids, all of whom know the Lord, are third generation. And I pray that the generations to follow continue in an unbroken line of godly faith.

A long time ago somebody told me that you never know how good a parent you are until you see your grandchildren. That can be a scary thought, but it can also be a great encouragement. When you live to see your grandchildren standing for the Lord and pressing on in the faith, suddenly all the toil and sweat and uncertainty and difficulties and anxious moments you endured as a young parent seem as nothing compared to the joyous vision that now kisses your eyes.

Was it worth it? Yes! Yes! A thousand times, *Yes!*

Christians enjoy the wondrous privilege of passing on their values to their children-but it doesn't happen merely because we profess faith in Christ. It happens when we live out our faith in a winsome and compelling way. When our kids see what a difference Christ makes in our lives, they will want Him to make that same difference in their own. As one author reported:

> *"Kids look to their parents to put the events of their lives—the ups and downs—in context. Mom or Dad have the opportunity to frame and give meaning to such occurrences. It takes a loving, attentive parent to take a common stone and make it into a milestone in a son or daughter's life."*
>
> **—Gary Smalley and John Trent**

Several years ago, a survey revealed that when Mom and Dad took (not sent) their children to church, 76 percent of the children followed their parents in their faith. If only the father took the children to church, the percentage dropped to 55 percent. Interestingly enough, if only the mother took the children to church, the percentage dropped to 15 percent. If neither parent took the children to church, only 9 percent became active Christians.[8]

Stop for a moment and take in those numbers. Seventy-six percent of the time when Mom and Dad bring their children to church, the kids become Christians. It is particularly hard for a young boy to become an avid Christ-follower when he sees it's not important to his father, the natural idol in his life. Seldom will a young man get excited about the faith if he doesn't see an excitement for God growing in the heart of his dad. I'm not guessing about this; I've seen it prove true countless times.

Yet if we take our kids with us to church–if we put into practice only this single principle–we would enjoy a 76 percent chance of seeing our children grow up to follow the Lord! That is astonishing . . . and it's far too good a deal to pass up. God has given us the opportunity to begin, with the kids under our roofs, a generational movement so bursting with divine power that it can shape a world that won't even exist for decades.

But it must begin with us.

Today.

Right where we are.

Victors instead of victims

Christian parent, have you thanked God for the opportunities He graciously gives you as a child of God? We have briefly looked at just three blessings that both the Bible and science say usually accompany a vibrant life of faith–good health, success in business, and the opportunity to pass on Christian values to your children–but those things alone should be enough to cause us to shout ourselves hoarse in gratitude.

I confess, I'm tired of Christians walking around with their heads down–as if there's nothing to rejoice about. I hear it all too often: "We're being picked on." "The world's a mess." "All hope for the righteous is gone."

Listen, we've known for a long time that we are the ultimate victors. Didn't the Apostle Paul say, "Now thanks be to God who always leads us in triumph in Christ"? (2 Corinthians 2:14) And didn't Jesus Himself tell us, "Come, you blessed of My Father, inherit the kingdom prepared for you from the foundation of the world"? (Matthew 25:34) Now add to that the mounting scientific evidence that proves *even in these present days* we are victors! We should be excited about that-and proud without arrogance.

We are children of the King! This life really is the good life! As Jesus said, "I have come that they may have life, and that they may have it more abundantly" (John 10:10). He wasn't talking about life someday, somewhere, in the great, misty by-and-by. He was talking about life right *here*, right *now!*

It's time for us to put our shoulders back and our heads up. When others start beating us up at work by casting insults in our face about our walk with Christ, we need to smile and say, "Oh, if you just knew what I know, you wouldn't be saying that. If you just knew what it was like to follow Christ and have the Holy Spirit living in your heart, if you just knew the power of prayer and all the other benefits that come with a commitment to pleasing God, you wouldn't say that."

It's time for us to walk tall in leading our families in the way of righteousness. It's time for us to revel in the grace God showers on our homes rather than focus on the strengths of the enemy. It's time for us to start acting like victors instead of victims.

Let's stop apologizing

As long as I'm on my soapbox, let me take a shot at another pet peeve. Christians are notorious for apologizing when something good happens to them. Have you noticed that? Have you ever run into a Christian who just bought a nice, new car? He describes the great deal he got, how it was just sort of dumped in his lap, how he knows he really shouldn't have this car, but.... By the time he gets done with all his explanations and justifications and apologies, all the joy of getting a new car has been stolen.

Why can't we just say, "God blessed me and I bought a new car"?

If we enjoy some success in this world, it is simply because the Lord is with us. God wants to bless His children and if He chooses to do so in our lives, we should fall on our faces before Him in gratitude, share our good fortune with others, and then enjoy to the full His wonderful blessing. But never, ever apologize! God is good and He loves to bless His children.

Not long ago I told someone that the previous three years of my life, including my bout with cancer, were the most wonderful years in my memory. God blessed me and my family in such a way that I could not begin to describe the whole of it. All I could do is look up into His loving face and say, "Thank You, Lord. You are a good God! Thank You for Your blessing. I am so grateful!"

Rejoicing comes in the morning

For good reason the Scripture says, "The blessing of the LORD makes one rich and He adds no sorrow with it" (Proverbs 10:22). Those who have committed their lives to Jesus Christ are the most favored and wealthy of all people–no matter how much money they have or don't have. And although sorrow may enter their homes for a moment, the Lord makes sure that tears will never win the day. "Weeping may endure for a night," says Psalm 30:5, "but joy comes in the morning."

That goes doubly, maybe triply, for Christian homes. We are not exempted from the ordinary trials and tribulations common to a fallen race, but we do have a divine promise that faithless men and women lack. God aims to specially bless those families who seek after Him with their whole heart, and He doesn't cover up what He's doing. His blessing lies out in the open, so plain that even secular researchers have no choice but to confirm the word of the Lord:

> Blessed is every one who fears the LORD,
> Who walks in His ways.
> When you eat the labor of your hands,
> You shall be happy, and it shall be well with you.
> Your wife shall be like a fruitful vine
> In the very heart of your house,
> Your children like olive plants
> All around your table.
> Behold, thus shall the man be blessed
> Who fears the LORD.
> The LORD bless you out of Zion,
> And may you see the good of Jerusalem
> All the days of your life.
> Yes, may you see your children's children
> (Psalm 128).

Gifts from God

---

1 Marianne K. Hering, "Believe Well, Live Well," *Focus on the Family* magazine, September 1994, 2.

2 Randolph C. Byrd, "Positive therapeutic effects of intercessory prayer in a coronary care unit population," *Southern Medical Journal,* July 1988; 81(7):826–29.

3 Christopher A. Hall, "Holy Health" *Christianity Today,* November 23, 1992, 18–22.

4 Florence Bulle, *God Wants You Rich and Other Enticing Doctrines* (Minneapolis: Bethany House, 1983), 41.

5 Korn-Ferry International Executive Profile: *A Survey of Corporate Leaders of the Eighties,* October, 1986.

6 Zig Ziglar, "The Importance of Family Involvement in Church," *Families,* ed.: Jerry B. Jenkins (Chicago: Moody Press, n.d.), 79.

7 Richard Thomas Bewes, "Our Spiritual Family Tree," *Families,* ed.: Jerry B. Jenkins (Chicago: Moody Press, n.d.), 180–184.

8 Zig Ziglar, "Parents as Role Models," *Families,* ed.: Jerry B. Jenkins (Chicago: Moody Press, n.d.), 76.

Five

Raising Courageous Daniels

"Do not be afraid, Daniel—Peace!

...Be strong now; be strong."

—DANIEL 10:12, 19 (NIV)

It's tough to live as a Christian in this world. It's hard to make good, godly decisions. But there comes the time and place when we are forced to make difficult decisions that shape the rest of our lives.

Some time ago I read a bit of advice from a father to a son who was about to venture into the world:

> You're starting, my boy, on life's journey.
> Along the grand highway of life,
> you meet with a thousand temptations.
> Each city with evil is rife.
> The world is a stage of excitement.
> There's danger wherever you go.
> But if you are tempted in weakness,
> Have courage, my boy, to say no.
> In courage alone lies your safety.
> When you the long journey begin
> Your trust in the Heavenly Father
> Will keep you unspotted from sin.
> Temptations will go on increasing
> As streams from a rivulet flow.
> But if you'd be true to your manhood,
> Have courage, my son, to say no.
> Be careful in choosing companions.
> Seek only the brave and the true.
> Stand by your friends when in trial,
> Not changing the old for the new.
> And when, by false friends you are tempted
> The taste of the wine cup to know
> With firmness, with patience, with kindness,
> Have courage, my boy, to say no.
> Have courage, my boy, to say no.
> Have courage, my boy, to say no.
> Have courage, my boy, have courage, my boy,

> Have courage, my boy, to say no.[1]

I doubt there's a parent who wouldn't like to sit his son down and say those very words to him. "Son, you're going to be thrown into situations where you will have to stand up for what's right. It's going to take guts to say no, but you'd better *learn* to say no if you want God to bless your life."

I wonder: If we parents could pass along only one character trait to our sons, what quality would we choose? What one single attribute, above all others, would we identify as paramount for our boys and young men? I submit that an excellent candidate would be courage.

The biblical imperative

Before King David died, he took steps to disciple his successor. First Chronicles 22:6-13 records how David prepared his son Solomon to follow him as leader of Israel–a wonderful picture of discipleship in every respect. The text describes David's efforts at discipling his son in the building of the temple as well as in the building of his son's character. Tellingly, he spends very little time talking about the building but a lot of time discussing the character of the builder.

In verse 12 David declares his concern that his son develop wisdom and understanding. In verse 13 he encourages Solomon to keep the law of the Lord God. Then at the end of verse 13 he sums up his instruction with these words: "Be strong and of good courage; do not fear nor be dismayed."

Six chapters later David is within days of taking his last breath, yet he's still singing the same tune. First Chronicles 28:20 reports, "And David said to his son Solomon, 'Be strong and of good courage, and do it; do not fear nor be dismayed, for the LORD God-my God-will be with you.'"

As David saw death approaching, the one quality he emphasized to his son–more than all others–was *courage*. David knew from his long years of ministry that Solomon would be tempted to cower from danger and shrink from the principles of God's Word, so he urged his son, "Don't do it! Be strong and stand true to the things of God."

The same pattern appears throughout Scripture. In the days when

Moses was handing off national leadership to Joshua, the Lord Himself said to the new leader, "Be strong and courageous. . . . Be strong and very courageous. . . . Be strong and courageous. Do not be terrified; do not be discouraged, for the LORD your God will be with you wherever you go" (Joshua 1:6–7, 9, NIV).

Centuries later when Assyria invaded Judah, King Hezekiah told his military officers, "Be strong and courageous; do not be afraid nor dismayed" (2 Chronicles 32:7).

To the Prophet Isaiah the Lord said, "Say to those who are fearful-hearted, 'Be strong, do not fear!' (Isaiah 35:4) and "Fear not, for I am with you; be not dismayed, for I am your God. I will strengthen you, yes, I will help you. I will uphold you with My righteous right hand" (Isaiah 41:10).

Through Jeremiah the Lord said to His people, "'Do not fear, O My servant Jacob, and do not be dismayed, O Israel!...Do not fear, O Jacob My servant,' says the LORD, 'For I am with you'" (Jeremiah 46:27-28).

The Prophet Ezekiel was given similar direction at the beginning of his ministry: "Do not be afraid of them, nor be dismayed by their looks" (Ezekiel 3:9). Even Daniel the prophet, one of the bravest men in the Old Testament, had to be encouraged: "Do not fear, Daniel. . . . Peace be to you; be strong, yes, be strong!" (Daniel 10:12, 19)

And such instruction isn't limited to the Old Testament. At the Transfiguration Jesus said to His top three disciples, "Do not be afraid" (Matthew 17:7). He repeated the same message to all His disciples after His resurrection (Matthew 28:10). The Gospel of Luke brims full of this admonition to courage: to Zechariah (1:13); to Mary (1:30); to the shepherds (2:10); to Simon Peter (5:10); to Jairus (8:50); to all the disciples (12:4, 7, 32).

A few years after His ascension Jesus appeared to the Apostle Paul

> *"How often do you mention the word courage around your kids? If your kids went into the Marine Corps, it would be part of the curriculum in basic training. If they were to become police officers or fire fighters, it would be part of their normal education. We can do the same thing. Courage can be part of our daily vocabulary."*
>
> **—Tim Kimmel**

and said to him, "Take courage!" (Acts 23:11, NIV) The divine message must have taken root, because just four chapters later the apostle delivered the same words to a group of frightened sailors: "I urge you to keep up your courage...so keep up your courage, men" (Acts 27:22, 25, NIV).

Throughout the Bible we find this instruction to God's people: *Don't be afraid! Don't be dismayed! Take heart! Take courage!* We're to stand on His Word, to be obedient to His will, to be wise in understanding-but in addition to it all, we're to be people of courage. The work is great and not for cowards.

This is a lesson for our families, in particular for our sons. And I can think of no better place to begin that lesson than by observing the life of Daniel and by drawing out several principles from his remarkable story.[2]

A captive in Babylon

In 605 B.C. Nebuchadnezzar, king of Babylon, besieged Jerusalem and removed several articles from the temple of God as well as approximately seventy "young men" from Judah's royal family and nobility. Daniel and his three friends, Hananiah, Mishael, and Azariah, were among the captives.

The Hebrew term translated "young men" in Daniel 1:4 normally denotes males from the age of fourteen to seventeen-youths mature enough to be taken from home, but young enough to be educated to new patterns of thought. When Daniel was carted off to Babylon, he was probably just fourteen years of age.

Immediately court officials immersed these captives into the Babylonian culture. The first thing Nebuchadnezzar did was change their names. In Hebrew, Daniel means "God is my judge"; it was changed to Belteshazzar, which means "the keeper of the treasure of Baal" or "Baal, protect his life." Hananiah's name, "Yahweh is gracious," was changed to Shadrach, which means "the command of Aku," a Babylonian moon god. Mishael, "who is like God?" became Meshach, "who is what Aku is?" while Azariah, "Yahweh is my helper," became Abednego, "the servant of Nego," another pagan god.

These boys were enrolled in the "University of Babylon" for a three-year crash course of study. At the end of this time they were to have learned the entire Chaldean language and all the wisdom of Babylon, including astronomy, astrology, and architecture.

Nebuchadnezzar intended to so immerse these young men in the culture of Babylon that nothing would remind them of their former life. He wanted them to forget Judah, forget the temple, forget their godly homes, forget all that was theirs as pious Jewish boys.

Think of it: a fourteen-year-old boy sent into a pagan culture, exposed to powerful, ungodly influences and made subject to intense pressure. Imagine sending your own fourteen-year-old son to the University of Beijing and abandoning him there to the teachings of Communist China, and you have some idea of Daniel's predicament.

Inevitably, the day came when Daniel was ordered to violate his conscience and abandon his commitment to God. His dilemma is described in Daniel 1:5: "And the king appointed for them a daily provision of the king's delicacies and of the wine which he drank." Yet somewhere along the way, Daniel had learned that it is never right to do wrong in order to do right.

Politely, respectfully, this fourteen-year-old refused to comply with the king's command.

Daniel could have said, "Now, wait a minute. I'm only a kid. I mean, after all, God, what do you expect? I haven't had a chance to mature in my faith." Or he could have said, "I'm away from home. I'm away from the temple, away from the ministers, away from my parents. I'm in a foreign land, hundreds of miles from home. Nobody will know." Or he could have said, "Lord, seventy-five of us came out here. How come only four of us don't get to eat the king's meat and the king's wine? Where are these other guys? They're Jews too. They come from the same culture we do. Lord, we're in the minority. That doesn't feel good. I don't like being in the minority. The peer pressure, Lord. . . ."

To add to his troubles, Daniel also knew that if he disobeyed, he wouldn't be around for long. He had heard the palace rumors. Nebuchadnezzar liked to play with fire, especially with human beings as the fuel. One of his favorite indoor sports was to throw people in the furnace. The Book of Jeremiah describes how Nebuchadnezzar forced observers to watch as he slowly roasted a man who displeased him.

Talk about a tough boss! That's the kind of vicious fellow the king was. So when Daniel thought about his decision, certainly he must have given thought to what might happen to him.

Despite all that, however, "Daniel purposed in his heart that he would not defile himself with the portion of the king's delicacies, nor with the wine which he drank" (Daniel 1:8). Quietly but firmly, he said no. He drew the line where God drew the line.

Now, remember that Daniel already had allowed the Babylonians to change his name; no fuss there. Nor did he fight his enrollment in Babylon University. But when they tried to feed him the king's meat and wine, he said no. At that point he courageously drew the line. Why?

The Old Testament contains no prohibition against taking a name from another culture. In fact, it often happened. It did so with Joseph, with Esther, and with many others. Likewise, there is no Old Testament prohibition against learning what other cultures have to teach. Moses did it (Acts 7:22 says that Moses was learned in all the wisdom of the Egyptians). So did Joseph.

But the Old Testament does strongly prohibit eating unclean food and meat offered to idols. So that is where young Daniel took his stand. Where God said no, Daniel said no. Period. He made up his mind to resist all the might of Babylon, all the threats of the most powerful man in the world, and every bit of worldly wealth and wisdom this planet had to muster. One young man stood up against all of that and said, "No! I won't do it." And he was only fourteen years old.

Oh, how we need sons in our day who are willing to follow Daniel's example! Immorality is wrong. Adultery is wrong. Fornication is wrong. God has drawn those lines very clearly. The world may try to blur the lines–or deny that they ever existed. But in God's Word, they're as clear as they ever were. If we want the blessing of God upon our sons' lives, we had better find the courage and the authority to help them stand, even as Daniel stood, and to say, even as Daniel said, "I will not defile myself because God has said no."

The courage of Daniel

As I study the book that bears his name, I notice at least five characteristics of Daniel's courage that I covet for my own sons.

1. He was uncompromising.

Daniel courageously said to one of the king's men, "Thank you for the invitation to eat at the king's table, but I have chosen to not defile myself with the king's food." When we take our stand and draw the line, it is like firing the furnace of our intestinal fortitude, enabling us to take the next step and be firm. If we can help our sons do that, we will give them the courage to take a stand when the test comes.

2. He demonstrated conviction.

Daniel championed a high standard against all forms of evil. He wanted to live way above temptation. He wanted to put his standard up so high that no one would have any trouble understanding his position.

3. He maintained his courtesy.

Had Daniel been a fightin' fundamentalist like some of us, he would have come across like Drano. He would have taken his stand in such a caustic, belligerent way that his comments would have wiped out every Jew in Babylon. Instead, this teenager simply resolved in his heart and presented his request that he might not defile himself. Walking in the power of an ungrieved Holy Spirit gives a person a kind of quiet strength.

4. He exhibited unflagging confidence.

Daniel believed in the Word of God. He knew his Lord would never let him down. So with confidence he said, in effect, "If God be for us, who can be against us?" He put himself on the line for what he believed. Daniel lived such a holy and righteous life, walking in the power God had given him, that he wasn't afraid to test his commitment before the whole kingdom. He demonstrates that holy living always brings confidence.

5. He maintained consistency.

Consistency may be the most difficult thing of all. Most of us have our good moments, but consistency is a hard quality to exhibit day after day.

After the dietary crisis blew over, Daniel 1:21 tells us, "Thus Daniel continued until the first year of King Cyrus." Daniel was not right just some of the time, or even most of the time. Daniel lived a consistently holy, righteous, godly life for over *seventy years* in the midst of the corrupt Babylonian palace.

Nebuchadnezzar came and went, but Daniel continued.

Belshazzar came and went, but Daniel continued.

Darius came and went, but Daniel continued.

By the time Cyrus rose to power, Daniel was still there, still God's man in the place of influence. He remained the same through it all. Calm. Clear-eyed. Consistent. Courageous.

The impact of Daniel

And what was the result of living like this? God rewarded Daniel with a special impact.

First, God gave him special influence *in the court.* The Scripture says he "served before the king" (Daniel 1:19). When Nebuchadnezzar saw how intelligent Daniel was and how well he had done in his course of study, the king brought him into the royal court. Ultimately he became prime minister of the kingdom.

Second, Daniel was influential *with his companions.* Can you imagine what it must have been like to count Daniel among your buddies? What must it have been like for Hananiah, Mishael, and Azariah to be close to Daniel? Do you think he had an impact on them? You bet he did! And we know this for certain by noting the stand *his buddies* took in Daniel 3 (more on that later).

Third, Daniel influenced *the captives.* Daniel remained their only consistent leader throughout the Captivity. Ezekiel provided a wonderful example, but he blazed on the scene for only part of the time. Can you imagine how the Jewish hostages in Babylon looked up to Daniel? "He's our man in the palace, he's our guy," they must have said. "Kings come and go, world powers rise and fall. But Daniel holds on to his integrity."

As far as I know, a phrase describing Daniel is repeated about no one else in the Bible: "O man, greatly beloved." The description is found in the Book of Daniel three times (Daniel 9:23; 10:11, 19). The only one who comes close to such a portrayal is the Lord Jesus Christ Himself.

Why was Daniel a man greatly beloved? He became the champion of his people in exile. The captives drew their strength from him, humanly speaking. They knew Daniel would be right. Who knows how many took their cue from him and committed themselves to following God with courage, come what may?

How to prepare a Daniel

How did God prepare Daniel to be the champion he was? What kind of home life produced a young man of such amazing courage and conviction? And how can we help our own sons to become modern-day Daniels?

God began His work in Daniel's life long before the Babylonian Captivity. Years before Daniel arrived at Nebuchadnezzar's palace–during his boyhood days–powerful forces deeply influenced Daniel.

In His providence, God allowed Daniel to be born during the reign of King Josiah. Josiah was the first good king Judah had enjoyed in fifty-seven years. Prior to him a wicked king named Manasseh had reigned for fifty-five years, succeeded for two years by his son Amon. Amon was so evil that servants in his own house conspired against him and murdered him.

Eight-year-old Josiah followed this awful mess to the throne. But 2 Chronicles 34 tells us that in the eighth year of his reign, Josiah began to seek after God. In the twelfth year he began to purge Judah and Jerusalem of its idols, and under his leadership one of the greatest revivals in history took place. With Josiah on the throne and Jeremiah in the pulpit, Judah fell to her knees and ultimately returned to God's blessing–if only briefly.

> *"Fathers help boys develop strong, healthy masculinity when the boys perceive them as the one who sets limits, makes decisions, controls disbursements of family capital, and administers discipline. Caution: these functions need to be undergirded with consistent affection and care-giving."*
>
> **—Dave Simmons**

While all of this was happening, little Daniel was running around, a prince in the royal court. There is good evidence he may have been related to King Zedekiah, and therefore very much a part of the inner workings of the revival. While we are told nothing of Daniel's parents, they must have been so involved in the reform under Josiah and

Jeremiah that when Daniel came to the palace in Babylon, he was ready to take his stand in an uncompromising way. God had been preparing him through all of those days for that moment when he would stand alone. And that, friend, must be our task with the sons under our roofs.

Standing up to peer pressure

Daniel lived a long time ago, but his example remains as fresh and relevant today as it ever was. Despite overwhelming pressures, this courageous teenager resisted evil and tenaciously clung to faith in the God of Israel.

As in any age, I'm convinced that one of the most potent pressures he had to overcome was peer pressure. Daniel had to withstand the constant urgings of the other seventy-odd Jewish captives to "go along with the program," to give in, to stop making waves, to get on board and make things safe for everyone.

Never doubt it, peer pressure is *powerful*-especially on those approaching adulthood.

The pressure to conform reaches its zenith when young people are moving from childhood to adulthood. During that time they care more about what their friends think than just about anything else. They feel insecure. They want to be accepted so badly that they become highly vulnerable to group pressure. That is why someone has said teenagers move in herds; they want to be a part of the group.

Dr. James Dobson tells of a team of doctors who conducted a telling experiment. Ten teenagers were brought into a room and told they were to be part of a study to evaluate visual perception. One by one, doctors held up a series of cards, each card featuring three lines, one line clearly longer than the other two. Students were to raise their hands when doctors pointed to the longest line on each card.

In fact, the doctors were studying the effects of group pressure. Nine of the ten students had secretly been instructed to vote for the second longest line every time the card was raised. In other words, they were to vote wrongly in every situation.

When doctors held up the first card and pointed to line A–clearly shorter than line B–nine of the ten students raised their hands. The fellow under study looked around in disbelief. How could this be? Line

B obviously extended further than line A. Yet he carefully raised his hand with the rest of the group. He later admitted that he thought, *I must not have been listening during the directions. Somehow I missed the point, and I had better do as everyone else is doing or they will laugh at me.*

The researchers then repeated their directions. "Vote for the longest line. Remember, now, vote for the longest line. Raise your hand when we point to the *longest* line." It couldn't have been more simple. They held up the second card, and again nine teens voted for the wrong line. The confused fellow grew tense over his predicament and eventually raised his hand with the group once more. Over and over, he voted with the group–even though he knew they were wrong.

Researchers repeated the experiment many times with different test subjects, and more than 75 percent of the "guinea pigs" voted with the group. Less than a quarter of the subjects tested had the courage to say the group was wrong.[3]

Such is the power of group pressure. Group pressure is one of the major reasons why kids try drugs and alcohol. In one survey, one out of ten kids said they took their first puff on a marijuana joint and their first sips of beer only to impress their friends.

"Come on, it'll be fun. Everyone's doing it," come the lines. "It's no big deal." "Are you chicken?" "If you were my friend, you would do this with me." "Trust me. We won't get caught." "I'm not going to invite you to my party if you don't do this with me." "You're a real wimp." "What a nerd." "Grow up!"

How can we help our sons to stay strong, to resist the tide, and follow Daniel's courageous example? Allow me to make six suggestions to enable us to get on top of the problem and develop a strategy to overcome it.

1. Teach your son to never underestimate the importance of his choices.

I'll bet the Old Testament character Caleb was one of Daniel's heroes. He's certainly one of mine. Daniel and Caleb had a lot in common. Caleb stood up for what he believed even when everyone else ran in a different direction. His story is told in Numbers 13 and Joshua 14.

Israel sent twelve spies into Canaan to determine whether the nation could take the land of promise. Ten of the returning spies whined, "We can't go in there. That land is filled with giants! We don't have anywhere near the power to overcome them. They are stronger than we are."

Caleb and Joshua had seen the giants too. But more than that, they had heard the promise of the Lord. So when Caleb returned, he stood up in front of all that dissenting, unbelieving crowd and said, "Let us go up at once and take possession, for we are well able to overcome it" (Numbers 13:30). The opinion of the ten cowardly spies prevailed, however, and the nation spent the next forty years wandering around in the wilderness.

Caleb was right; the majority was wrong.

A single bad decision—one poor choice made in the heat of passion—cost the Israelites a whole generation. Because of their unbelief, they were sentenced to die in the wilderness. Not one of them, except for Caleb and Joshua, was allowed to see the Promised Land. On the flip side, Caleb's courage to stand up for what he believed changed the course of his whole life and that of his family.

Sometimes we think, *It doesn't make any difference what I choose this time. It's just one decision, just one choice.* To that C.S. Lewis says:

> Every time you make a choice you are turning the central part of you, the part of you that chooses, into something a little different from what it was before. And taking your life as a whole, with all your innumerable choices, all your life long you are slowly turning this central thing either into a heavenly creature or into a hellish creature; either into a creature that is in harmony with God, and with other creatures, and with itself, or else into one that is in a state of war and hatred with God, and with its fellow-creatures, and with itself.[4]

Help your son to see the critical importance of his choices. *Every choice he makes in some way changes what he is inside.* Every time he decides against God and against good, he does something to himself that makes it easier for him to respond wrongly the next time. And every time he decides for God and for good, he builds something into his inward character that will help him become who he ought to be.

2. Help your son to decide his convictions before he faces the choice.

The back seat of a car is no place for a young man to determine how he feels about sexual purity. He'd better have made that decision long before he steps into the vehicle.

The Bible never hints that Daniel and his friends struggled with what to do when they were offered the king's wine and meat. They already held firm convictions on the matter. Daniel didn't have to start from scratch and scribble out a game plan to meet the crisis. He already knew that eating from the king's table would violate who he was before God. He made his choice long before the choice had to be made. Good policy!

Encourage your son to get his convictions from his love for God and from His Word. Urge him to memorize Scripture verses that will strengthen him when the pressure comes. But most of all, help him to make the right decision before it has to be made. That way, when the crisis comes he will simply be enforcing a decision, not making one–and it is much easier to enforce a decision than to make a tough choice under pressure.

> So use every piece of God's armor to resist the enemy
> whenever he attacks, and when it is all over, you will
> still be standing up (Ephesians 6:13, TLB).

3. Train your son to determine the risk factor in every situation.

Proverbs 1:10-16 sounds like it could have been written for our culture today:

> My son, if sinners entice you,
> Do not consent.
> If they say, "Come with us,
> Let us lie in wait to shed blood;
> Let us lurk secretly for the innocent without cause;
> Let us swallow them alive like Sheol,
> And whole, like those who go down to the Pit;
> We shall find all kinds of precious possessions,
> We shall fill our houses with spoil;
> Cast in your lot among us, let us all have one purse"–

My son, do not walk in the way with them,
Keep your foot from their path;
For their feet run to evil,
And they make haste to shed blood.

It happens every day. An ungodly group tries to recruit a new member by saying, "Come be a part of us. Hey, we're going to do this caper. We're going to do this thing. Come on! Throw in your lot with us." But God, through the writer of Proverbs, says, "Don't even walk in their way. Don't go near them. Don't walk in the area where you can be tempted to join them. They are headed for evil and you need to scope it out so you don't even get close to where they are."

Every one of us is smart enough to know where trouble lies. When your son's heart starts sending him signals that something looks a little shady, that's his warning. Train him to get out, fast. Walking into a high-risk situation makes no sense for anyone who wants to stay clean and true in the things of God. Train your son to ask himself, "Is this a place where I belong? Is this the kind of thing I need?"

4. Show your son how to depend on God every day.

I honestly believe that peer pressure has become so overpowering today that no teen can cope with it apart from the Lord. If your son doesn't depend on God with all of his heart, if he doesn't ask God to give him the strength he needs to stand up and be counted, if he doesn't realize that God is his ally and walks with him every day, he will risk a ruined life. He cannot possibly make it through the teen years without God.

Here is where I think of Daniel's three friends, Shadrach, Meshach, and Abednego. In chapter 3 of his book, Daniel has moved out of view and his buddies have taken center stage. King Nebuchadnezzar built a huge golden idol to which everyone in the kingdom was supposed to bow down and worship. And everyone did. Except these three teens.

Do you realize how badly you stick out of a crowd when everyone is bowing down while you're standing up? Suddenly these three young men found themselves in big trouble. They knew that if they didn't bow down, they would be thrown into a fiery furnace.

How did they respond when the thermostat got turned up? I love their words in Daniel 3:16-17: "O Nebuchadnezzar, we have no need to answer you in this matter. If that is the case, our God whom we serve is able to deliver us from the burning fiery furnace, and He will deliver us from your hand, O king. But if not, let it be known to you, O king, that we do not serve your gods, nor will we worship the gold image which you have set up."

In other words, they were saying, "We stand here with God on our side. If we are thrown into the fiery furnace and that's God's will, so be it. And if we survive the fiery furnace and that's God's will, so be it. But understand this, Nebuchadnezzar: We don't care about the penalty or the circumstances. We're going to do what's right. We are going to stand for God because God stands for us." In the end God did rescue them—and the only thing that got burned were the ropes that tied these boys together!

> *"When a boy has a father who has modeled tenderness, it will be much easier for that boy to give the same tenderness and understanding to his children when he becomes a father."*
>
> **—Steve Farrar**

It delights my heart when I hear of young people who, every day when they get up, read their Bible and pray, "God, help me to be Your person today. Help me to have courage." God is on the side of those who take His side.

And do you know what kind of teens are most likely to have such a brief time with God in the morning? Teens with parents who model such a time for them. When you get up in the morning to spend time with God, your son will likely follow suit.

5. Encourage your son to develop friends who will stand with him.

Until our children became teenagers, I never realized the full importance of their choice of friends. I've noticed that the men in the Bible who stood strong for God often stood with others. Such friendships aren't hard to recall: Paul and Silas; Peter and John; David and Jonathan; Paul and Luke; Joshua and Caleb; Moses and Aaron; Daniel and his three friends. And isn't it interesting that in Luke 10 when the Lord sent out a group of seventy-two disciples, He sent them out two by two? There is great strength in even one ally.

Remember the study on teens and group pressure I described earlier? The same test was repeated later, with one key variation. Researchers found that if only one other student voted for the right line, the chances significantly improved that the "guinea pig" would stick by his choice of the correct line and vote against the eight others. The message to teenagers is clear. In Dr. Dobson's words, ". . . if you have *even one friend* who will stand with you against the group, you probably will have more courage too."[5]

Remind your son that many years from now it won't matter if his friends were popular or athletic or "in." What will matter is their commitment to God. If your son develops friendships with others who want to please God, those friendships can strengthen and help him as he moves through the difficult teen years.

6. Motivate your son to declare his decisions with courage.

Like Daniel, Joseph faced temptation at every stage of life. He stood alone against his brothers. He stood alone against the promiscuous culture of his day. He stood alone when his boss' wife said to him, "Lie with me." Genesis 39:8 tells us simply, "But he refused."

"Absolutely not!" he said. "No way!" Of course, there are all kinds of ways to say no. Here are just a few:

- No, thank you.
- Thanks, but no thanks.
- Don't think I will.
- I'll pass.
- I'm not really interested.
- Definitely not.
- No, I want to live.
- That's wrong.
- I'm afraid not.
- Can't.
- Uh-uh.
- That's dumb.
- Don't want to.
- Don't think so.

- Next year. Remember to ask me then.
- Are you crazy?
- Nope. Not if I want to see tomorrow.
- Forget it.

One author I read suggests using humor to say no. When someone asks your son to do something he knows he shouldn't, he can say:

- Sorry! I have to get home to walk by pet piranha.
- Great! I'm supposed to do something with my pastor tonight. Can he come too?
- I'd love to, but I have to refill the ink in all my pens.
- Sorry. If I did that, I might fit in with your group better!
- Love to, but I'm expecting to get *Beanie Baby Monthly* in the mail today!
- Sounds fun, but that's the same night as my cricket lesson.
- No thanks, I'm planning to finish building the Sistine Chapel with Lincoln Logs.
- Love to, but I am color-coordinating my shoelaces tonight.
- It's my night to watch the grass grow. Sorry!
- Oh, rats! Can't. My all-state croquet team has practice.
- Wish I could! But I threw my boomerang and I have to wait for it to come back.
- Sure, and right after that, let's jump into an erupting volcano!
- I'd like to, but tonight I'm counting the watts in all the lightbulbs.

Motivate your son by personal example to say no to ungodliness. And do it with conviction. Don't do it apologetically. Say it with strength. You have every right to do it. You are standing on the authority of the

Word of God. You have nothing to be ashamed of. What you believe in is what you ought to believe in. God is good and you have determined to follow Him, regardless of how many others run in the wrong direction. You can't stop them if they want to go, but you don't have to accompany them. And neither does your son. When it's called for, say no with a sense of conviction–and motivate your son to do the same.

Who remembers them today?

Seventy-five hostages came out of Jerusalem and were taken to Babylon. Daniel, Meshach, Shadrach, and Abednego are four of them. Can you name even one of the others? I'll bet not. Why not? They're forgotten and gone. Ditto with the spies who accompanied Caleb and Joshua into the Promised Land. You can't give me the name of one other person in that group, can you? Why not? Because they're all long gone and forgotten.

But the men who stood up will be remembered forever!

The desire for popularity now often puts at risk being remembered later. The people with the guts and the courage to stand up for what they believe are the people who rise to leadership. Neither you nor your son can make something out of your life without the courage to swim upstream once in a while, to say no when everybody else is saying yes.

Daniel is an example to all of us, regardless of what we do or where we live. We need not bend the rules to be blessed of God. Success does not depend on compromising our commitments. Daniel's influence came not because he broke the rules, but because he refused to budge when God said no. I believe our world is hungry for a few men who will stand up and say, "I'll be like Daniel. I'll stand as he stood. I'll draw the line where God draws the line, no matter what."

A young man entered a state university. During the first few weeks of class, a godless professor asked if any students considered themselves to be Christians. It was obvious the professor was trying to embarrass anyone who dared to raise a hand. One young man looked around and saw that none of the other 200 students would admit to their faith, even though he knew of other Christians in the room. What should he do? He either had to admit his Christianity or deny it like Peter did when Jesus was about to be crucified.

This young man suddenly held up his hand and declared boldly,

"Yes. I'm a Christian." The professor made him stand in front of the class and said to him in a voice dripping with sarcasm, "How could you be so stupid as to believe that God became a man and lived here on earth? That's ridiculous. Besides, I read the Bible, and I'm going to tell you, it didn't do a thing for me."

The young man looked the professor straight in the eye and said, "Sir, the Bible is God's letter to Christians. If you don't understand it, that's what you get for reading someone else's mail."[6]

Neither we nor our sons have to take a back seat to the world. We don't have to be dragged along the path to destruction. We can teach our sons to have the guts to stand up and be who they are before God. They don't have to succumb to peer pressure. By the grace of God, your son can grow up to be an overcomer.

Just like Daniel.

---

1 Author unknown. Quoted in David Jeremiah, *The Handwriting on the Wall* (Dallas: Word Publishing, 1992), 37–38.

2 The following material on the life of Daniel originally appeared in a more summarized form in my book, *The Handwriting on the Wall* (Dallas: Word Publishing, 1992).

3 Dr. James Dobson, *Preparing for Adolescence* (Santa Ana, Calif.: Vision House Publishers, 1978), 46–49.

4 C.S. Lewis, *Mere Christianity* (New York: The MacMillan Company, 1966), 86.

5 *Preparing For Adolescence*, 46–49.

6 Ibid., 62–63.

Six

Rearing Faith-Filled Esthers

"Then Esther told them to return this answer to Mordecai:

'Go, gather all the Jews who are present in Shushan,

and fast for me; neither eat nor drink for three days,

night or day. My maids and I will fast likewise.

And so I will go to the king, which is against the law;

and if I perish, I perish!'"

—ESTHER 4:15-16

ale Evans Rogers has written several books of interest about her family and life. In one chapter titled "What Is a Girl?" she gives a tender description of a daughter:

> Little girls are the nicest things that happen to people....
> A girl is Innocence playing in the mud, Beauty standing
> on its head, Motherhood dragging a doll by the foot.
> God borrows from many creatures to make a girl.... He
> uses the song of the bird, the squeal of a pig, the stub-
> bornness of the mule, the antics of a monkey, the
> spryness of a grasshopper, the curiosity of a cat, the
> speed of a gazelle, the slyness of a fox, the softness of a
> kitten.... She is the loudest when you are thinking, the
> prettiest when she has provoked you, the busiest at
> bedtime, the quietest when you want to show her off,
> and the most flirtatious when she absolutely must not
> get the best of you again.... Who else can cause you
> more grief, joy, irritation, satisfaction, embarrassment,
> and genuine delight than this combination of Eve,
> Salome, and Florence Nightingale?[1]

Who, indeed?

Daughters have a unique way of bringing into our homes the full glory of life in all its grandeur and grief. Daughters, every bit as much as sons, have the potential to do great things for God. And it is our privilege and duty as parents to help them achieve all they can in Christ.

Amy Carmichael, who became "mother" to hundreds of destitute Indian girls who otherwise would have spent hopeless lives as temple prostitutes (or worse), once wrote a prayer for teenage children:

> Dear God, make them good soldiers of Jesus Christ. Let
> them never turn back in the day of battle. Let them be
> winners and helpers of souls; let them live not to be

ministered to, but to minister. Make them loyal; let them set loyalty high above all things. Make them doers, not mere talkers. Let them enjoy hard work and choose hard things rather than easy. Make them trustworthy; make them wise for it is written: God has no pleasure in fools. Let them pass from dependence on us, to dependence on Thee. Let them never come under the dominion of earthly things; keep them free. Let them grow up healthy, happy, friendly, and keen to make others' happy. Give them eyes to see the beauty of the world, and hearts to worship its Creator. Let them be gentle to beast and bird; let cruelty be hateful to them. May they walk, O Lord, in the light of Thy countenance. And for ourselves we ask, that we might never weaken. God is my strong salvation. We ask that we might train them to say that word, and live that life, and pour themselves out for others, unhindered by self.[2]

> *"Children who come from homes with accurate moral compasses will be clear as to who they are and what they are to do."*
>
> **—Steve Farrar**

I especially prick up my ears at Amy's last petition: "We ask that we might train them to say that word, and live that life, and pour themselves out for others, unhindered by self." Who wouldn't love to have a daughter of whom it is said, "She poured herself out for others, unhindered by self"? Such a daughter would be a rare jewel in anyone's crown. But notice: how do our daughters become such women of faith?

By being trained.

By whom?

By us!

A selfless young woman

A prime example of the sort of woman Amy Carmichael prayed for is found in the Old Testament book of Esther. Whatever training young Esther received at home, it enabled her to became a woman who "poured herself out for others, unhindered by self."

Esther, you'll recall, was a stunningly beautiful and godly Jewish woman of the fifth century B.C. God used her to save her people and thus preserve the family line through whom the Messiah, Jesus, eventually came.

Esther grew up as an orphan in the home of her cousin, the godly Mordecai. He reared her as his own and she lived under his roof until the day she was chosen to "audition" to become the wife of King Xerxes ("Ahasuerus" in the Hebrew) of Persia. Out of all the eligible young women summoned to the palace, Esther was chosen to replace Queen Vashti, who had been deposed after she publicly humiliated her husband. And so the Lord positioned one of His people in a strategic place so that when an evil man named Haman hatched a plan to annihilate the Jews, Esther was there to stem the tide.

As in the life of Daniel, we lack specific information regarding what child-rearing techniques were used to produce such an extraordinary woman of faith. Nevertheless, certain hints so consistently appear throughout the narrative that we can confidently extrapolate some of the most important principles on how to rear a godly Esther.

How to rear an Esther

We are told that "Mordecai had a cousin named Hadassah, whom he had brought up because she had neither father nor mother. This girl, who was also known as Esther, was lovely in form and features, and Mordecai had taken her as his own daughter when her father and mother died" (Esther 2:7, NIV).

Mordecai was a kindly man who reared his uncle's daughter as his own. We get a poignant picture of his loving and caring nature in Esther 2:11. By this point in the story Esther has been taken to the palace as a candidate to become the king's wife. And Mordecai, who had watched over his cousin since she was a tiny girl, every day "walked back and forth near the courtyard of the harem to find out how Esther was and what was happening to her" (NIV).

I visualize a man who knew he had put a young girl in a place of danger, where he was no longer able to care for her needs. While he apparently realized he had done so by the purpose and will of God, he could not even for a day cease to think of her and wonder how she was doing.

Some scholars have suggested he had access to this house where the women were kept because he was involved to some degree in the Persian government. The Bible does say he sat at the city gate, a place where a judge might conduct his business. But regardless of his governmental position, Mordecai continued to show his love and concern for Esther even after she left his house.

And Esther responded to his love! She knew Mordecai could be trusted and leaned heavily on his wisdom. That is why she complied with his instructions not to reveal her Jewish identity at first. Esther 2:10 says, "Esther had not revealed her people or kindred, for Mordecai had charged her not to reveal it."

Even after Xerxes chose Esther as queen, she continued to obey Mordecai's word: "Now Esther had not revealed her kindred and her people, just as Mordecai had charged her, for Esther obeyed the command of Mordecai as when she was brought up by him" (Esther 2:20).

Remember, Esther was now the queen. The coronation party had been thrown. She had been established. All of the other women had been dismissed. She was now enthroned in the royal palace. No more powerful woman existed in all of the land. Yet the Bible says she continued to keep her identity a secret, even from her own husband. Mordecai had told her, "Don't tell him yet," and even though she ruled as queen, she still showed allegiance to the man who reared her. She still cared what her earthly father thought. She wanted to do exactly what Mordecai had asked her to do.

Why had Mordecai given such an instruction? It seems obvious that if Esther had immediately revealed who she was, her part in the contest for a new queen would have ended before it started. God knew what He was doing, and He allowed her to ascend to the throne by keeping quiet about her nationality.

Such is the home Mordecai and Esther shared. Mordecai loved his foster daughter, cared for her, and instructed her carefully. In turn, Esther returned her cousin's love by honoring him and obeying his instructions. And while we are not given a peek through the window to see what else little Esther might have been taught to prepare her for the crisis to follow, by her actions we can safely deduce the kind of instruction she received in Mordecai's home.

She sought the Lord

When Mordecai warned Queen Esther that her life and the lives of her kinsmen were in danger, he asked her to go before her husband the king and persuade him to change his mind. This was a fearful request, for two reasons.

First, in the Persian court a person did not come unbidden to the throne. If someone were to dare approach the king without being summoned, he or she must be executed–unless the king raised his scepter to indicate he would grant the unscheduled audience. Esther didn't have just a little bit to lose if she blew this assignment; she had her head to lose.

Second, according to Persian custom, once the king had enacted a law, even *he* could not change it. He could not make a law one day and undo it the next. Once he proclaimed the law, even he was bound by it.

So how would Esther respond? Esther 4:16 tells us she asked Mordecai to call together all the Jews in her community to pray and fast for her for three days, and she and her servants would do the same. She sought the Lord to intervene. She prayed, asking God to soften the king's heart before she ever spoke to him.

Now, where did Esther learn about prayer? Where did she learn about fasting? Where did she learn that God was her strong fortress in time of trouble, her immovable rock in the howling storm? The obvious answer: at home, with Mordecai.

That's why I'm sure of one thing. Despite the gravity of the situation, as Mordecai left Esther that day to carry out all of her instructions, I believe he wore a satisfied smile. His foster daughter had learned her lessons well!

She exhibited godly wisdom

After sending Mordecai to mobilize the prayer team, Esther waited for most of three days before approaching the king. She didn't want to set foot in the palace without at least three solid days of prayer and fasting behind her.

The Bible says that once she did approach the king, "she found favor in his sight, and the king held out to Esther the golden scepter that was in his hand. Then Esther went near and touched the top of the scepter. And the king said to her, 'What do you wish, Queen Esther? What is your request? It shall be given to you–up to half my kingdom!'" (Esther 5:2-3)

What would you have done at that moment? Blurt out what you wanted? Spill all of the beans? Would you have said, "All right, King, if I can have whatever I want, what I want is Haman dead. I want his head. I want him killed right now. And I want all this anti-Semitism stopped."

But Esther was reared to be wiser than that. She was a woman of great restraint. She had a blank check from the king, but she did not tell him what she desired. Instead, she invited the king and Haman to a special banquet. She intended to get her husband in a good mood, to put him in the best position to get what she really wanted. She set up the king in the most beautiful and majestic way.

Here is the heart of a godly, wise woman fully played out and documented for us to study. She is going to put Xerxes in a position where he cannot but say yes. Esther understood that her husband loved high living. He was a banqueting king, a royal party animal. She also knew that he highly valued Haman. So she played right into the king's interests. A ravenous, grouchy lion can be transformed into a contented pussycat after a nutritious meal.

And her wily ways didn't stop there.

Once Xerxes attended her banquet and asked again that she name her request, Esther replied, "My petition and request is this: If I have found favor in the sight of the king, and if it pleases the king to grant my petition and fulfill my request, then let the king and Haman come to the banquet which I will prepare for them, and tomorrow I will do as the king has said" (Esther 5:7-8).

By now the king's curiosity had reached fever pitch. *A second banquet? What could she possibly want? What's on her mind? What a mystery! What fun! What a woman!*

Not until the following day at the second feast did Esther finally tell her husband what troubled her. Perhaps he expected her to ask for half the kingdom, for palaces full of treasure, for wardrobes stuffed with designer clothes from all over the known world.

But no. She asked simply for her life:

> If I have found favor with you, O king, and if it pleases your majesty, grant me my life-this is my petition. And spare my people-this is my request. For I and my people have been sold for destruction and slaughter and annihilation. If we had merely been sold as male and female slaves, I would have kept quiet, because no such distress would justify disturbing the king (Esther 7:3-4, NIV)

"Fathers play a strong role in their daughters' future sexual adjustment. Women who had a strong, stable relationship with a loving father usually find the adjustment to mature femininity much easier. They are usually more secure in their sexual nature and they find it easier to love their husbands."

—Peter Blitchington

Now, how do you think the most powerful man on the planet would react to such news, to such a deadly threat to his treasured wife? What else would he do but explode in rage and demand to know the identity of the man responsible for Esther's peril? Imagine how Haman must have felt when he heard Esther report, "The adversary and enemy is this vile Haman." In short order, Haman was hanged, the Jews were given permission to defend themselves, and Mordecai (who earlier in the story had saved Xerxes' life from an assassination plot) was elevated to a position of great power.

And the key to Esther's success? She helped Xerxes to both understand and feel how this crisis threatened his own happiness. She displayed great wisdom, cunning, and humility, and carefully avoided anger or retribution. She made sure her remarks never embarrassed her husband or caused him to lose confidence in who he was. Everything she did prepared his heart to understand.

Now, where does a young woman gain that kind of poise? Where does she develop such insight and confidence? How does she come by such a fine sense of timing and drama? The obvious answer once more:

at home, with Mordecai. It was he who instilled all these godly qualities in young Esther as she grew into a woman of faith.

And it seems to me that every one of those qualities grew out of the
rich, deep soil which covers every speck of land in this book: an
unshakable faith in the absolute sovereignty of God. If we want to rear
our own daughters to follow in Esther's remarkable footsteps, we must
help them to walk on the same solid ground that she did.

Focus on God's sovereignty

Did you know Esther is the only book in the Bible that never once
mentions the name of God? And yet the will and power of our
Almighty Lord permeate that book like almost nowhere else in
Scripture. In many ways, Esther is the perfect book for demonstrating
the sovereignty and providence of God. For while His face is nowhere
seen, His hand is everywhere present.

Think about Esther growing up without a mother or a father.
Apparently they died early on. It was difficult for Esther, I am sure.
Those who have grown up in single-parent families can tell you that
God may give a mother or a father enough love almost to make up for
two—but never quite. Sometimes those difficult circumstances can be
painful and hurtful and they prompt us to wonder, *God, is there anything
You can do? Why can't I see Your face anywhere?*

Before the Lord called me to preach, I thought for certain that I
would find a job in radio and television. Toward that end I took several
college courses. My friend Paul Gathany and I also started WCDR, a
twelve-watt radio station in Cedarville, Ohio, broadcasting from the top
floor of the college administration building. On a good day you could
hear it on the second floor. (Today it's a hundred thousand-watt station
with translators all over the state of Ohio.) During my junior and senior
years I actually became an FM disk jockey in Springfield, Ohio, for a
couple of years. But then God called me to preach.

Yet even after I went off to seminary in Dallas, I drove up to North
Texas State University and took two courses in radio and television
production. When finally it became clear to me that God had called me
to the ministry, and not into radio or TV, all my radio work seemed to
be a long, useless detour. I thought, *I was sure God wanted me involved in*

radio, so I prepared for that in good faith. But now that door is closed. What in the world…?

Today, as the host of a nationwide radio ministry called *Turning Point*, I look back and realize God was orchestrating all of my training long before I knew what I would be doing. I didn't know back then how useful my training would be.

But God did.

Every event in my life has played a part in God's plan for me, even the difficult things. His will was at work in my life even when I didn't understand it, even when I struggled against it. Often God works out His will in our lives not because of us, but in spite of us. Difficult circumstances never frustrate God's will.

A few years ago Ken Poure and I were speaking at Hume Lake, a Christian conference center. Several times that week Ken told a story about his cute little granddaughter. A Sunday School teacher had asked her students to describe God. What could they say about Him? Ken's granddaughter piped up and said, "God is somebody who never says, 'Oops!'"

There are no accidents with God. He never says, "Oops!" God didn't wake up this morning and say, "Oh, my goodness, I forgot about you guys! And look what a mess you've gotten yourselves into." I don't have a God who is on vacation. I don't have a God who wakes up and has to turn on CNN to find out what's happening across the world. No, God knows all about us and our circumstances. When we realize that, we can take courage to do the right thing. God's sovereignty encourages us to do that right thing, even in difficult situations. We can look out on the landscape of our lives and realize God is in charge. Nothing ever surprises Him.

That is a lesson Esther had to learn. When Mordecai learned of the annihilation edict engineered against the Jews by Haman, he tore his clothes as a sign of mourning and sent a message to Esther informing her of the crisis. But she hesitated. She knew she could not approach her husband without first being summoned, and she hadn't been summoned for thirty days. How could she speak with the king? Mordecai didn't want her to die, did he? The following response made clear Mordecai's position:

> Do not think in your heart that you will escape in the king's palace any more than all the other Jews. For if you remain completely silent at this time, relief and deliverance will arise for the Jews from another place, but you and your father's house will perish. Yet who knows whether you have come to the kingdom for such a time as this? (Esther 4:13-14)

Throughout history people have asked themselves and others, "Why am I in this mess?" I'm sure Esther must have wondered why she ended up in the situation that threatened her. What an impossible dilemma! She felt caught in the middle. All the friends she so dearly loved had fallen under sentence of death. Her foster father implored her to plead their case before the king, but she resisted because it might cost her own life. So Mordecai responded like this: "Esther, dear, you really have but three options. Let me spell them out for you.

"Option #1: You can be destroyed. Just because you're the queen doesn't mean you won't be executed, once the ax starts to fall. When they find out you're a Jew, you will be eliminated along with the rest of us. That's the law of the Medes and the Persians, and it can't be changed.

"Option #2: You might be passed over. Esther, you might be God's answer, but don't imagine you're the only possibility. If God doesn't deliver us through you, He'll use someone or something else. You could be THE answer, but you might not be the only answer. Do you really want to be passed over?

"Option #3: Sweetheart, you may have been born for such a time as this. Maybe God has placed you right in the center of this situation so you can be God's person, the Lord's chosen means of deliverance. Yes, it's uncomfortable-but God has called us to be faithful, not comfortable."

And then, all alone, Esther had to make her decision.

Responsibility and sovereignty

Some people get the wrong idea about God's sovereignty. They think that it somehow exempts them from tough personal decisions. But what happened to Esther? Was she brought to the kingdom "for such a time as this?" Absolutely! But that didn't excuse her from making decisions, even hard, agonizing decisions. She had to decide, "Am I going to walk in before Xerxes and plead the case for my people, or am I not?" God didn't just swoop down from heaven and force Esther to do the right thing. The decision was left to her. And in Esther 4:15-16 she makes the decision of a lifetime:

> Then Esther told them to return this answer to Mordecai: "Go, gather all the Jews who are present in Shushan, and fast for me; neither eat nor drink for three days, night or day. My maids and I will fast likewise. And so I will go to the king, which is against the law; and if I perish, I perish!" (Esther 4:15-16)

I'm not sure how much of what Esther said in that last phrase was prompted by spiritual reflection. Maybe she simply had sorted out the options and determined that in eleven months she was going to die anyway, so she might as well take the risk and try to escape death and hope that God was indeed in this whole thing. But whatever she meant, her words have come down to us with great power. Many books have taken as their titles, *If I Perish, I Perish,* reminding us that our survival isn't the only important issue. The crucial thing is that we cooperate with God Almighty, making ourselves available to Him so that He can use us wherever we are, whatever the situations we face.

In church we sometimes sing the little chorus, "In Times Like These." I'm sure Esther did not understand why she landed in this precarious situation. What a tough place to be! But she *could* find encouragement in the sovereignty of God. It appears Mordecai must have taught her that everything that comes into our lives passes first through the hands of our loving Heavenly Father. And when we know that, even when the difficult days come, we can be encouraged. There is great encouragement in good doctrine!

Still, the sovereignty of God exempts no one from personal decisions. Esther's words, "If I perish, I perish," are filled with the agony of her own personal choice to do what she believed God wanted. In God's sovereignty, Esther really *was* born "for such a time as this." But she demonstrated the correct response to sovereignty when she said, "I'm going to do what God wants me to do. And if I perish, I perish."

What does this mean for you and your daughter? Just this: Let God worry about His sovereignty, and you take care of your responsibility. If you or your daughter have a decision to make, don't hide behind the sovereignty of God and say, "God is in control so I don't have to do anything. I'll just wait and see what God is going to do." No, you must come to grips with biblical principles and make the decisions you need to make.

God sometimes puts us in tight places we don't understand. But if we believe that there are no accidents with God and if we are walking in obedience to His will, we can take great comfort in knowing that the God who created us and gave us new life through His Son Jesus Christ will not allow anything to happen to us outside of His sovereign control. Thank God, the Lord almighty is sovereign! And that fact can give us and our daughters the confidence to do what is right, even when doing what is right may seem as scary as walking the rail around the Grand Canyon.

Everyone is important

Does God's sovereignty make you feel small? It really shouldn't. The sovereignty of God actually exalts the importance of each individual. Did you ever think you're not important? Did you ever wonder how, in this world so overloaded with people, you could have any meaning whatever? If you have been plagued by such thoughts, think again of Esther's story.

Esther, in the right place at the right time, making the right decisions in obedience to God, by *herself* stemmed the tide. The actions she took as an individual-one lone, young woman-prevented the destruction of the Jewish nation and vouchsafed the redemption of you and me. Remember, Jesus came out of the lineage of the Jews, and had the Jewish nation perished in Persia, the house of David would have burned to the ground, eliminating the Messiah before He could be born.

Esther may not have realized when she was made queen the awesome responsibility she had inherited. Yet the fact is, just one person-just one somebody, just her-changed the course of world events.

One person *can* make a difference. A huge difference. Consider what a solitary individual may accomplish:

> In 1645 one vote gave Oliver Cromwell control of England. In 1649 one vote cost Charles I of England his life, causing him to be executed. In 1776 one vote gave America the English language instead of the German language. In 1839 one vote elected Mark Morgan governor of Massachusetts. In 1845 one vote brought Texas into the Union. In 1868 one vote saved President Johnson from impeachment. In 1875 one vote changed France from a monarchy to a republic. In 1876 one vote gave Rutherford B. Hayes the United States presidency. In 1923 one vote gave Adolf Hitler control of the Nazi party. In 1941 one vote saved the Selective Service Agency just one week before Pearl Harbor.[3]

Don't tell me one person doesn't make a difference! The sovereignty of God exalts the importance of just one person, because God uses everybody in His plan. He has no throwaways. Nobody is meaningless in the providence of God.

You are important, and so is your daughter.

Tell her that. Reinforce that truth. Prove it to her from Scripture. Teach her that people look to her for inspiration—that what she says and what she does really make a difference in people's lives. As she walks before God, as she expresses her love for the Lord every day, she impacts the world around her. And that isn't just pleasant talk or wishful thinking; it is what the sovereignty of God teaches us.

She cannot say, as Esther tried to say at the beginning, "I can't do anything about it." Yes, she can.

She can do what God calls her to do.

She can start where she is.

She can stand up and be counted in the issues she cares about.

She may not be able to change everything in the world, but in the context of her life, God can help her to make a difference. He is sovereign and everybody counts with God.

Final lessons from a courageous queen

Our daughters may never face the kind of national crisis that confronted Esther...but they will have to deal with personal dilemmas that seem just as huge. How can they face their own fierce battles with an unwavering commitment to God? I think the life of Esther leaves us with three final principles.

1. The more crucial the project, the more critical the preparation.

Esther did not waltz into her initial audience with the king without preparing herself–and without using all her Jewish friends to help her prepare. In effect, she got on the phone and called her prayer chain. She asked her kinsmen to fast for three days, even as she did. She knew she needed to prepare for the critical moment. Our daughters must learn the same lesson.

As I read the New Testament, I am reminded that the night before Jesus chose His twelve apostles, He prayed all night. Why did He do that? Because this was no small step. Even the Son of God wanted to pause, connect with His Father, and make the right choices. He knew better than anyone that the more crucial the project, the more critical the preparation.

Sometimes we think that time spent in spiritual preparation is wasted. When the effort seems indirectly related to the end objective, we wonder if we are riding a bicycle without a chain, if we are perhaps spinning our wheels. As a famous football coach has said, "While there is no shortage of athletes with the will to win, there is a shortage of athletes with the will to *prepare* to win."

We all want victory. We all want to have our audience with the king and come out triumphant and get what we requested. But we and our daughters must learn from Esther that the more crucial the project, the more critical the preparation. It is no waste of time to prepare spiritually for the moment of the big decision, to face the difficult challenge. It is a crucial time in the accomplishment of God's will.

2. While waiting on the important issues, we can still work on the mundane.

Sometimes we mistakenly imagine that waiting means going into suspended animation, absolute inactivity, motionless passivity. Esther's life puts the lie to that belief.

The first time Esther appeared before Xerxes to plead for her people, she invited Haman and the king to a banquet that "I have prepared for him" (Esther 5:4). For three days prior to this she had been fasting and preparing a banquet for her husband. Imagine that–putting together a sumptuous feast while you yourself have tasted nothing for seventy-two hours. Doesn't sound like much fun, does it? If you have ever been on a diet while still preparing "normal" dinners for the rest of the family, you know something of the agony involved.

For three days Esther prepared a banquet for King Xerxes and for Haman while she ate nothing herself. Was she waiting? Sure. But while she waited on the important issue, she worked on the mundane things that needed to be done. Our own daughters must master this lesson.

If you would rear your daughter to be an Esther, you must teach her that life goes on even as she waits on momentous events. "Normal" life cannot stop simply because homecoming approacheth. Homework must be done even though her church youth group is about to take a short-term missions trip to Africa. Home responsibilities continue even when Prince Charming is returning home from college for a weekend visit. While she waits on the important issues, she can still work on the mundane.

3. When her cause is righteous, her courage will be reinforced.

Esther had a righteous cause. She was to stand for her people by appearing before the king and pleading for the life of her race. Was she afraid? There is zero doubt about that!

But courage is not the absence of fear; courage is persevering in the face of fear. Courage doesn't mean we are oblivious to the danger. Courage may mean that we truly understand the danger, but in spite of that we go forward (sometimes with our knees trembling).

If Esther had waited until she had everything together, if she had been unwilling to walk into that inner court and make herself visible to the king and thereby risk her life, she never would have accomplished what the biblical record tells us she did.

In fact, we probably never would have heard of her. She would have been just one more person among the billions who was born, lived for a moment in the sun, then passed away into dust.

But Esther faced her worst fears and in the power of God stepped forward in great courage. And some two and a half millennia later, we're still speaking her name.

A young woman in a moment of crisis who waits to act until she gains all the courage she needs will never act. It simply won't happen. But if she has the courage to take the first little step, God will reinforce her courage and give her greater strength to complete the task.

I know it is enormously difficult to continue to uphold righteous convictions when everyone else is heading in the opposite direction. Christian young people who truly love the Lord often must feel like a fish swimming upstream. And the people who are passing them going downstream are their Christian buddies!

But if we teach our daughters to know and to do what is right, in the process of doing what is right, God will reinforce their courage and move them from courage to courage. Discourage your daughter from thinking she should wait until she can say, "Now I know I have enough strength." Encourage her to take the righteous step *now*, to move in the righteous direction *now*, to do what she knows God wants her to do *now*—and in doing so she will be reinforced with the courage she needs to continue, step by step.

> *"When daughters receive the esteem-building attention and intimacy with dad, they learn to feel comfortable with masculinity and will relate well to their male peers, pick a good husband and be a good mother to a son."*
>
> **—Dave Simmons**

They can grow bigger

In 1922 a British adventurer by the name of George Leigh Mallory led an expedition to conquer Mount Everest. The first expedition failed. The second expedition failed. Then with a team of highly qualified and hand-picked people, Mallory made a third assault in 1924. Despite careful planning and extensive safety precautions, the third attempt to climb Mount Everest ended in disaster. An avalanche killed Mallory and most of his party.

When the few survivors returned to England, they held a glorious banquet saluting the brave people of Mallory's final expedition. As the leader of the survivors stood to acknowledge the crowd's applause, he looked around the hall at the framed pictures of Mallory and the six comrades who died with him in their attempt to climb the never-before-scaled peak. Then he turned his back to the crowd to face a huge picture of Mount Everest behind the banquet table, looming like a silent, unconquerable giant. With tears streaming down his face, he addressed the mountain on behalf of Mallory and all of his dead friends.

"I speak to you, Mt. Everest, in the name of all brave men living and those yet unborn. Mt. Everest, you defeated us once; you defeated us twice; you defeated us three times. But, Mt. Everest, we shall someday defeat you, because you can't get any bigger and we can."[4] (Incidentally, seventy-one years later, in the summer of 1995, George Leigh Mallory's grandson, George Mallory of Austraila, made it to the Everest summit.)

The challenges of life will not get much bigger than they are right now. But by helping your daughter to build her faith in God, she can grow into a spiritual giant able to face any crisis with strong faith in a sovereign God. If you teach her to do the right thing today by following a righteous cause, she will be given the courage to face the next challenge. God builds our faith little by little, adding a little more spiritual muscle every time we do the things that seem difficult. In that way we and our daughters gradually gain the strength to do the really hard things that inevitably come to us.

In the great Persian crisis, Esther found the faith in a sovereign God to do what her foster father Mordecai had prepared her to do. Because of that, even to this day, her memory is honored and revered in the Feast of Purim. Even as Jewish revelers twirl noisemakers and stamp their feet at every mention of Haman's name, they bless Esther for her wise and selfless actions.

Could your daughter be another Esther? You bet—as long as she has a Mordecai or two to train her in the way of God and hold her accountable to make the tough, courageous choices "in such a time as this."

---

1 Dale Evans Rogers, *Time Out, Ladies!* (Westwood, N.J.: Fleming H. Revell Co.), 1966, 55–56.

2 Source unknown.

3 Paul Lee Tan, ed., "The Historic One Vote," *Encyclopedia of 7700 Illustrations* (Rockville, Md.: Assurance Publishers, 1979), 620.

4 James S. Hewett, ed., *Illustrations Unlimited* (Wheaton, Ill.: Tyndale House Publishers, Inc., 1988), 131.

Seven

Pride and Joy:
A Two-Way Street

"Parents are the pride of their children."

—PROVERBS 17:6 (NIV)

"The father of a righteous man has great joy;

he who has a wise son delights in him."

—PROVERBS 23:24 (NIV)

*O*ne of Norman Rockwell's famous paintings shows a beaming father looking down on a proud son who has just smashed his way through a row of would-be tacklers to score a touchdown in a big game-leaving a few of his teeth behind in the process.

You can't help but smile when you see this warm-hearted snapshot of days gone by. Something deep within us revels in family scenes where parents delight in their children, and where those children take pride in Mom and Dad. Rockwell's painting helps us feel the attraction of precious words like "unity" and "harmony" and "healthy pride" and leaves our hearts brimming with light and sunshine.

In real life, two anonymous parents from Texas must have combined forces to create just such a family scene. A few years ago one of their lucky daughters wrote to columnist Ann Landers to express her gratitude for her delightful heritage:

Dear Ann Landers:

I have read so many letters in your column from people who have no respect, let alone love, for their relatives. This one will be different.

When my mother died three years ago, she left a small amount of disability insurance that was divided in equal amounts among her six children. Since our eldest sister had taken care of Dad for eight years and then cared for Mom until she passed away, I felt that she should have my share of the money.

You can imagine how happy I was when I arrived at my sister's home and found that my brother had already sent her his check. He had decided quietly on his own, as I did, that our sister who took care of Dad and Mom should have his share of the inheritance.

Mom left no big estate. There was just the old house where we were all born and the little property it sat on. The property, with every family member's consent, was sold immediately after the funeral. The proceeds were divided between that wonderful eldest sister and another sister who had never married. Our unmarried sister had lived in apartments most of her life, and we decided that she should have a little home of her own. We all had dinner together one night and my brother greeted Sis like this:

"Well, they're breaking the ground for construction on your home. It will be down the block from us."

"Home? What home?" she asked.

"YOUR home, Sis. Congratulations!"

There was a lot of whooping and hollering and a few tears. It was a thrill for us just to see the look on her face.

Last week I received a check in the mail from my unmarried sister. It was my share of Mom's government bonds. I called Sis and told her I was returning the check to her. She said, "You can't do that. My feelings will be hurt." Can you imagine? She insisted that I take the money, buy something lovely for my daughters and tell them it was from their grandmother, purchased with the last bit of money she had left behind for us.

Ann, we are not wealthy people. We are all underpaid Texas teachers who have always lived from paycheck to paycheck, but I consider myself very lucky to have been born into a family that is so loving and generous.

I know this letter is too long to publish, but I did have a lot of fun writing it.

-R.A. in S.A.

To which Ann replied:

Dear R.A.:

What a terrific upper. After reading thousands of letters from family members who are at war over money, it's a privilege to print a letter like yours. Too bad your parents didn't leave behind a book on how to raise children.[1]

Wouldn't you love to leave behind such a legacy of kindness and generosity? With God's help, you can! Fortunately for all of us, the Lord *did* leave behind a book on how to raise children. It's called the Bible.

Entering a two-way street

A pair of verses from the Proverbs looks at healthy families from divergent perspectives. The second half of Proverbs 17:6 (NIV) says, "parents are the pride of their children," while Proverbs 23:24 (NIV) declares, "The father of a righteous man has great joy; he who has a wise son delights in him."

You know you've found a healthy, happy family when the children in that home take pride in their parents. Not only are they unashamed of Mom and Dad, they brag about them to their friends. They include them in their plans. They crave their guidance and their approval and they take every opportunity to "show them off."

Yes, families like this may be rarer than they once were, but they still exist. They're still possible. And your family can be one of them.

Family pride is meant to go both ways, however. That's why the second Proverb tells us that fathers delight in wise sons. Every father can be his son's (and daughter's) biggest cheerleader. Of course, it's equally true that mothers exult in wise daughters (and sons)! The point is that in healthy, godly homes, respect and admiration travel on a busy two-way street. When parents delight in their children, their children usually return the favor. When a father or mother show pride in their son or daughter, the child responds by looking up to Mom and Dad. It's a glorious two-way street no home in the world should live without.

But what's the secret to building such a two-way thoroughfare? How do you create such a happy home? Is there a proven way to establish a household in which parents delight in their children, who in turn take pride in them?

I think there is. And the key is found in another two biblical texts not explicitly about child-rearing. But read them for yourself:

Imitate me, just as I also imitate Christ (1 Corinthians 11:1).

> "The healthiest fami-
> lies I know are the
> ones in which the
> mother and father
> have a strong, loving
> relationship between
> themselves. This
> seems to flow over to
> the children and
> even beyond the
> home. The strong
> primary relationship
> seems to breed secu-
> rity in the children,
> and, in turn, fosters
> the ability to take
> risks, to reach out to
> others, to search for
> their own answers,
> become independent,
> and develop a good
> self-image."
>
> —Dolores
> Curran

Join with others in following my example, brothers, and take note of those who live according to the pattern we gave you (Philippians 3:17, NIV).

To some ears, these words of the Apostle Paul sound overconfident. Even arrogant. But the truth is, all of us learn far more by example than we do by lectures and exhortation. Paul lived so close to the Father that he was unafraid to say to young believers, "Watch how I live, then imitate what you see. I'm your role model. I don't expect you to do what I say if I don't live what I say. So observe how my colleagues and I operate. Take notes, if you like. Then mimic what you see. You need role models, and God has put me and my companions in your life for that purpose. Follow me as I follow Christ. Let's do it together."

Parents, in exactly the same way, God has put us in our children's lives to be their role models. It's a big part of our jobs…maybe the biggest part. Of course, the assignment is difficult, almost impossible. Yet that is precisely God's plan for moms and dads who want to delight in sons and daughters, who in turn look up to them.

The awesome power of parental role models

Modeling is incredibly important in the process of parenting. We learn far more from what we see in our home than what is said there. Long after our children have forgotten what we have said, they will remember what we do.

Images–both negative and positive, pleasant and unpleasant–will be burned into their memories for a lifetime.

The way parents treat their children in daily living has far more impact on their children's spiritual development, for example, than any of the family's religious practices, including having a regular family altar, reading the Bible together, and attending church services regularly. Why? Because everyday life merely illustrates our real convictions. Jesus said, "For out of the abundance of the heart the mouth speaks" (Matthew 12:34). And it is equally true that out of the abundance and overflow of the heart, the legs walk and the hands move and the eyes watch. We go places, do work, and watch activities that line up with our bedrock convictions and basic desires.

Recently I read a book titled *What They Did Right*. The author, Virginia Hearne, interviewed thirty-eight "celebrity" Christian couples and their children about what these famous moms and dads did right. Over and over again the same message came through:

"They lived the Christian life before me."

"They were models of good people."

"They were consistent in their Christian convictions."

It wasn't what these famous parents said that most impressed their children. These sons and daughters didn't talk much about economic prosperity or poverty. They didn't gush about their parents' success. They simply said their moms and dads were genuine, real people who lived out at home what they claimed to believe. Does that mean they made no mistakes? No. But when they failed, they dealt with their mistakes in an honest way.

The testimonies of these young people merely confirm that what we say is not nearly as important as who we are. Parents communicate acceptable lifestyles far more by modeling than by speaking.

If I were to travel anywhere in the country and take a survey of men and women who have grown up knowing the Lord, statistics say about 80 percent of them would report they came to faith in Christ because of their parents. They would say, "My parents had a strong influence on my life." That's certainly true of me and my children.

A relationship with God is not taught nearly as much as it is caught. Our walk with the Savior becomes infectious in our family as our children begin to see that what we say we believe has a real impact on how we *really* do live day by day. In other words, it isn't window dressing. It isn't a costume we slip into on Sundays. *It's the real thing.*

Gifts from God

A vital, genuine relationship with God cannot be taught in a classroom. It can never be taught around a table reading the Bible. As important as those things may be, a relationship with Christ is taught only as our children see it lived out in front of their eyes.

We cannot impart what we do not possess. If our children are to come to faith and live out strong moral principles and forge lasting commitments, they must see these things first take place in us.

Good role models, great results

One of the greatest encouragements to be an effective role model is to see what good parents can mean to a son or daughter. Consider the impact that just a few mothers and fathers (and one grandma) had on their own children.

The daughter of Winston Churchill wrote on one occasion, "The greatest and the most powerful influence in my life was of course my father. Although I had talked with him so seldom, and never for a moment on equal terms, I conceived an intense admiration and affection for him; and after his death, an affection for his memory. I read industriously, almost every word that he had ever spoken, and I learned by heart large portions of his speeches. He seemed to own the key to everything, or almost everything worth having."[2]

Here was a young lady who saw in her father "everything worth having." What a role model he was for her!

Luan Zemmer Jackson will forever be grateful for the influence of her grandmother. In an article titled "Mrs. McGillicutty's Band-Aids," she recalls her early days as the daughter of a poor country pastor. She and her family lived in a small house without running water or indoor plumbing and depended on the kindness of generous parishioners for food and clothes. Life was hard, but Luan remembers most the gift of her grandma, who lived across the road. Every day Luan would dress up in her best outfit and knock on her grandma's door, where she would be greeted as if she were the most important, most special person in the world.

In one of their many games the pair would pretend to be neighbors; Grandma was Mrs. McGillicutty and Luan was Mrs. Zemmer. Day after day they would enjoy high tea and talk about their families (Luan's grandma had six children; Luan had her dolls). Rainy days were the enemy; they made Luan "a prisoner at home and kept Grandma's world out of reach."

She writes:

> On one occasion, after several days of rain, I persuaded my mother to let me go to Grandma's. As I crossed the road, I fell into a massive mud puddle. Sitting in that cold, murky water, covered with slimy mud, I started to cry. Embarrassment and shame overwhelmed me. How could I have been so careless? My good dress was filthy. My knee was scraped and hurting. What would Grandma say?
>
> From her yard on the other side of the road, Grandma saw my plight, came across the road, and rescued me. With a smile she said, "Don't cry, Luan, we'll get you all cleaned up. Your dress will be fine and we'll put a Band-Aid on that knee."
>
> Grandma talked to me as she cleaned my wounds. "Luan, I want you to remember how embarrassed you feel-and how your knee hurts. Other people hurt some-times, too. It feels good to have someone take care of you, doesn't it? Remember that others have hurts and need to be cared for."
>
> After that incident I became a "ministering angel." I started a doll hospital. My friends played house with their dolls, but I had a new mission-to help people who needed my services....
>
> Grandma helped me envision an exciting and fulfilling future. "When you grow up," she said, "you will be a great nurse, because nurses are caring just like you and they take care of hurting people just like you do." In between sips of tea, she complimented me on my communication skills and encouraged my sense of humor. "In a world full of pain, we need to laugh and help others to laugh," she would say with a chuckle.[5]

Are you surprised to learn that Luan became a nurse and today owns and operates a full-service mental health clinic? What power we parents (and grandparents) have as role models for our children!

Indira Gandhi, the daughter of Nehru and a former prime minister of India, has been regarded as one of the outstanding women of this century. Let me tell you what most shaped her life.

One biographer wrote, "Although both parents were strong examples of intense loyalty to their motherland, it was her father's influence that formed the pattern for her life as a leader."[4] Nehru took a keen interest in his daughter's education and encouraged her to read and think for herself. While he was away, the pair carried on a great dialogue through the mail. Later, those letters were published. When India became independent from Britain and Nehru was elected prime minister, Indira served as his hostess and later participated in policy-making and vital decisions.

But a story dating from before India's independence moves me the most. After Indira married and gave birth to a son, authorities arrested her father and intended to transfer him from one prison to another. Indira's baby was only a few months old and his grandfather had never seen him. She learned the car bearing her father would use a certain bridge. And so at dusk, wearing a sari which her father had woven for her, she stood in a visible spot near the bridge and lifted the baby high above her head so that Nehru could catch a glimpse of his grandchild. What a poignant picture of her love and affection for the man who had made such an impact upon her life!

Indira's father wove more than a sari for her; he designed the very fabric of her life. More than anyone else, he shaped her life and future.

Valerie Elliot Shepard is the daughter of Elisabeth Elliot, the former wife of missionary Jim Elliot, who was slain more than forty years ago by the Auca Indians while trying to bring the Gospel to this fierce South American tribe. Some time after her husband was killed, Elisabeth brought her family back to the Aucas to continue the work her husband began.

Valerie wrote, "My mother believed God brought us to the Aucas to share the good news with them. Every night when she put me to bed, she sang and prayed for us. I always felt completely secure and safe. I still remember two special songs from those childhood years in the jungle–'Jesus, Tender Shepherd, Hear Me,' and 'The Lord Is My Shepherd.'

"Perhaps the most important gift from my mother was that she instilled in me a confident trust in my heavenly Father. She believes and lives the promises of God."[5]

What stayed most with Valerie about the training she received in her growing up years? Her mother "believes *and* lives" the promises of God. In other words, she's an effective role model.

Grammy Award-winning singer Michael W. Smith has said he hopes he can be as consistent with his own kids as his dad was with him. "I always saw my dad reading the Word," he recalls. "And if he wasn't working and the church doors

"I have come to the conclusion that the best way I can improve my children's spiritual lives is to continually improve my own."

—David Mains

were open, he was there. Dad didn't talk to me a lot about God, not as much as I do with my kids, but he was dedicated in everything he did. There was never any doubt in my mind about my dad's convictions, because his actions proved them." And then he writes:

> The most important lesson I learned from my dad is to remember to say "I love you" even in the down times. Even when your kids are rebelling, just keep saying it.
>
> I'll never forget one particular time when Dad told me he loved me. I'd been down in Nashville, living out of God's will, just breaking his heart. In the middle of this rebellious time, we got on the phone and he told me that he loved me, and I told him that I loved him.
>
> I got off the phone and thought, *Man, that's incredible. He told me he loved me.*[6]

Michael's dad wasn't afraid to *show* his son that love, either. The musician says his best memory of his dad was created during his "The Big Picture Tour" in '86 and '87. "He's proud of his son, probably a little too proud," Michael said. "But just to see him enjoy that music at the concert was so cool.[7]

Michael Smith's father unknowingly embodied the wisdom described in the book *Lifetime Guarantee:*

> Boys become men by watching men, by standing close to men. Manhood is a ritual passed from generation to generation with precious few spoken instructions. Passing the torch of manhood is a fragile, tedious task. If the rite of passage is successfully completed, the boy-become-man is like an oak of hardwood character. His shade and influence will bless all those who are fortunate enough to lean on him and rest under his canopy.[8]

Mothers, too, can provide a lot of shade for their children under the canopy of their love. In an article titled "Mother's Hospitality," Nancy Groom meditated on her penchant for hosting company, despite the inconvenience, and asked herself, *Why do I keep doing this?* Then she remembered her mother. Her mother and father were to visit for Christmas and Nancy phoned to see if they were ready to come.

> "Well, not quite," my mother admitted. "I talked to Uncle Ernie yesterday, and he said your cousin Janice and her four children are coming here to visit him for Christmas. They planned to stay in a motel for the week, but I told him they're welcome to stay at our house while we're gone. Right now I'm straightening things up and getting some food ready for them."
>
> "If that isn't just like you, Mother!" I said with a laugh, shaking my head. "You've always opened your home to those who need it-it's one reason I love you so much."....
>
> When we got off the phone, I reflected fondly on my mother's typical kindness. All my life I'd observed her working overtime to provide pleasant experiences to delight and refresh others.... Why should I have been surprised that before leaving for her Florida

Christmas she would try to make a Michigan Christmas "homey" for my cousin and her family?

And why should I be surprised that I, too, enjoy opening my home to those I love and who need my care? *Maybe hospitality is in my genes,* I thought.

More likely, I have learned to share my heart and my house by having seen my mother's kindness oft repeated with no thought of repayment. She and my father will surely recognize more than a few angels when they get Home, for they have welcomed many a stranger, many a time.[9]

There's the refrain once more: "I learned to share my heart and my house by having seen my mother's kindness oft repeated." What our children see in us, they imitate. Even as adults!

A second Ann Landers column proves again the power of a father committed to living out the code of conduct he preaches to his kids. When dads model for their children a loving, consistent lifestyle, this is what can happen:

Dear Ann Landers:

I read an article recently in the *St. Louis Post-Dispatch* about teaching values to our children. The writer said, "If there is a simple way to instill in children the qualities that will keep them happy and help them contribute to the world while doing no harm to others, I have not found it."

Well I HAVE found it–by imitating my father. He taught me by example. He went to work every day and was home to have dinner with us in the evening. He had a strong faith in God. If he could help someone in need, he did. He was always considerate of his parents and treated my mother with respect.

My dad grew up in the Depression and went to work to help support the family before finishing eighth grade. He was a side gunner in World War II. Once, while visiting my grandmother in the nursing home, he found a $5 bill on the sidewalk and turned it in at the office.

My father taught me honesty, respect, courage, faith, responsibility and kindness. I thank God every day for giving me such a fine role model. I am happily married to a man who is very much like my dad. We will celebrate our 15th anniversary next month. We have four children. I hope I can instill the virtues in my children that my dad taught me.

-Peggy in O'Fallon, Illinois

Ann Landers wrote back:

Dear Peggy:
Your letter bears testimony to the fact that children learn by example. If you and your husband adhere to this formula, it should work again. Thank you for a letter millions of parents can learn from.[10]

Finally, consider the wise mother briefly described by Jean Fleming in her book, *A Mother's Heart*. Fleming tells of Gordon Parks, the youngest of fifteen children born to a poor Kansas farmer. Parks never completed high school, yet authored several books, directed films, composed a symphony, and wrote several sonatas. Fleming says Parks attributes his many accomplishments to his mother, Sara Parks, "a poor, uneducated black woman who often had a Bible tucked under her arm.

"Just before her death when Gordon was fifteen, she called him to her and said, 'Son, I think you're going to be a great man. But I want you to work at it. Mind your sisters. They'll tell you what is right because I've taught them what is right. Then go north. Take advantage of everything. Do things a little better than the best. Do things a little bigger than the biggest. But always remember this place-I want this house to be your learning tree.'"[11]

Gordon Parks succeeded not because he enjoyed wealth or social standing. He had neither. Gordon Parks succeeded because of a mother who fulfilled her central place as a role model. Sara Parks may have been uneducated, but the "learning tree" she provided for her son continues to bear fruit to this day.

That is the influence of a godly parent. That is the wondrous effect a dedicated mom or dad can have on an impressionable son or daughter. And that is the world-changing power of a role model.

We can't fake it

We can't fool our kids. At home, you and I are the real you and I. "Do as I say, not as I do," won't cut it. What we do is so powerful that it can destroy everything we say, as the following sad poem reminds us:

> He whipped his boy for lying,
> And his cheeks were flaming red,
> And of course there's no denying,
> There was truth in what he said.
> That a liar's always hated,
> But the little fellow knew,
> That his father often stated,
> Many things that were untrue.
> He caught the youngster cheating,
> And he sent him up to bed,
> And it's useless now repeating,
> All the bitter things he said.
> He talked of honor loudly,
> As a lesson to be learned;
> And forgot he boasted proudly,
> Of the cunning tricks he'd turned.
> He heard the youngster swearing,
> And he punished him again,
> He'd have no boy as daring,
> As to utter words profane.
> Yet the youngster could have told him,
> Poor misguided little elf,
> That it seemed unfair to scold him,
> When he often cursed himself.

All in vain is splendid preaching,
In the noble things we say,
All our talk is wasted teaching,
If we do not lead the way.
We can never by reviewing,
All the sermons on the shelves,
Keep the younger hands from doing,
What we often do ourselves.[12]

We had better live out what we say we believe from the Word of God, or our words will act more like poison than fertilizer in the soil of our children's hearts. On occasion I hear parents say, "I want my children to grow up in the church even though I'm not into church." But why would our children grow up in a way contrary to how they have been reared? Our kids will watch and imitate what we do and will throw away what we say.

"Make their life together a sign of Christ's love to this sinful and broken world, that unity may overcome estrangement, forgiveness heal guilt, and joy conquer despair. Amen."

—The Book of Common Prayer

Some years ago, I copied these words in the flyleaf of my Bible: "Whatever parent gives his children good instruction, and sets for them at the same time a bad example, may be considered as bringing them food in one hand, and poison in the other."

Across the years of my ministry I've talked to countless young people who have rejected the faith of their parents. In these discussions one consistent truth has come out: while their parents talked the truth, a very large gap yawned between what they said and how they lived. More than one young man has told me, "I went to church as long as my mom made me, but as soon as I got old enough to make my own decisions, I cut out."

"Why did you do that?" I ask.

"Dad never went, so it must not be a manly thing to do. If Dad doesn't have to go to church, then I don't have to go to church. So when I could make my own decisions, I didn't go, either."

You can't fake it. Nobody can. I certainly can't. If we don't model a real, genuine relationship with Jesus Christ, there is little chance our children will grow up to possess what we lack.

You can choose to say, "I don't want my children to be Christian." You can choose to say, "I do not wish to impact the morality of my children." But you may not say, "I want my children to grow up Christian with high morals and great integrity" and then violate all those principles in your own life. We never get anything other than what we sow. The only basis for a return on investment is what we invest in the first place.

Luke 6:40 says, "A disciple is not above his teacher, but everyone who is perfectly trained will be like his teacher." This means that once we have trained our child, he or she will be just like us. That's a sobering thought. As much as we sometimes hate to admit it, our children reflect us and the dynamics at work in our home. So what do we do if we don't like what we see in our children?

Charles Swindoll asks, "Don't you think it would be easier to change you than to try to change two, three or four children? If you are the one who is causing all this, instead of trying to change all of them, why don't you change you and then, when they see you, they will change. Is it easier to change one person, or four people (especially if you are the one who needs to change)?"[13]

For many reasons King David is revered by millions even today, centuries after he ruled Israel. He gave his children all they needed-except an example they could follow. As you trace the pattern in David's family, you see David's children repeating the same lifestyle mistakes their father made. His serious errors stripped him of the power to restrain his children.

The same thing happened with Lot in Genesis 13–19. Lot left Ur with Abraham, his uncle. They owned so many goods they couldn't take care of them together, so they separated. Lot was given his choice of land and settled near Sodom. Before he knew it, he was seated at the gate of Sodom.

Some of the saddest words in the Bible are recorded of Lot and his progeny. When God decided to judge Sodom and Gomorrah, He sent a warning to Lot, who took it to his married daughters. They had married men from Sodom–and these wicked men laughed in Lot's face (Genesis 19:14). Lot had gained much in real estate, but had lost all influence with his own family.

Or I think of a man named Eli, a priest in Israel who served and sacrificed before the Lord but who failed to meet God's standard for effective parenting. In 1 Samuel 2:12 we read this description of Eli's sons: "Now the sons of Eli were corrupt; they did not know the LORD."

Eleven verses later we read that Eli confronted his sons with the words, "Why do you do such things? I hear from all the people about these wicked deeds of yours. No, my sons; it is not a good report that I hear spreading among the LORD'S people" (1 Samuel 2:23-24, NIV).

Eli's sons were committing adultery at the very door of the tabernacle where Eli ministered. Yet Eli did not know firsthand what his boys were doing; he had to depend on outside reports. On the basis of those reports he confronted his children. So we have to ask the question, "Where were you, Eli?"

Probably the worst statement that could be made of any father is found in verse 25 (NIV): "His sons, however, did not listen to their father's rebuke, for it was the LORD'S will to put them to death."

Here is a priest, perhaps over-committed, doing the work of God—but he'd lost influence in his own family. Eli reminds me that I must never stop doing my work at home in order to continue doing the work of the ministry. My priorities need to be clear. Am I getting too busy with other things so that my children are being neglected? It is important for all of us, no matter where we are in the parenting process, to stop for a moment and examine how we're dealing with our children.

Does this mean we have to be perfect? Of course not. None of us are. I can't be perfect and I'm not. My children know all my failures. I've made hundreds of mistakes in my family. But when I know about them, I admit them and we go on. My children see the genuineness of who I can be in Christ as I trust the Lord each day.

I want my kids to see the genuine article in me. That's my heart's goal and prayer. And I know you want the same thing for your own family.

The older, the better?

I believe young people today are looking for an older generation of adults who can prove by their lifestyle that life is worth living, no matter how many candles light up the birthday cake.

Years ago I heard someone say that the devil didn't have many happy old people. And I thought, *Yeah, and God doesn't have as many as He should, either.*

Have you noticed how many people grow up-and grow mean? Instead of maturing and demonstrating to the next generation how to handle the advance of years, they grow grouchy and cranky. Sure, we can't do some of the things we used to and we don't move at the same speed–but we can still be fun people. We don't have to get mean, old, and grouchy. We can become godly, loving, and fun.

I know growing older itself isn't fun. That's why there's so much humor about getting older. I hear them all the time:

> "You know you're getting older when everything hurts and what doesn't hurt doesn't work."
>
> "You know you're getting older when you sink your teeth into a steak and they stay there."
>
> "You know you're getting older when you see a pretty girl walk by and your pacemaker makes a garage door go up."
>
> "You know you're getting older when you bend down to pick something up and your mind says, *Is there anything else I should do while I'm down here?*"

Of course it's all right to age; none of us can help it. But we don't have to get *old*. I know of many keen-minded aged people who are very young. And fun!

Our young people need to understand that we've learned enough about the grace of God in our journey with the Lord that we've begun to internalize what we've been telling them for so many years. They want to see if it really *works*.

By the grace God, I want to be a fun person for my children and their families. I want to be an aged person who's not getting old. I want to be the kind of a person who's continually growing so that my children can see what life is supposed to be like when a person gets up in years. I want to be a good role model even as I begin to saddle up for a long ride off toward the sunset.

Gifts from God

Footprints amid the debris

Many years ago when we lived on the East Coast, every summer we used to spend two weeks in Ocean City, New Jersey. A church family owned a duplex right on the ocean, and every August they handed us the keys to their house and said, "It's yours for two weeks."

I have photos showing us dragging down to the ocean all the paraphernalia required when you have little ones. From the cottage door to the ocean we lugged a bassinet and a crib and buckets bulging with toys—it seemed like hundreds of miles. We left in the morning and stayed all day because it was too hard to come back. We didn't want to do it more than twice a day.

Every evening after dinner we took a walk on the beach. We spent many hours walking the beautiful, white sandy shores. One night we decided to stroll to the boardwalk, about twenty blocks away. It was 7 P.M. when we started toward the city; low-tide was to be at 7:30, and the ocean was busy depositing its debris on the sand, the ugly along with the beautiful. The whole bunch of us walked in bare feet and we had to be careful not to step on broken shells or, worse, jelly fish. I gave the children a stern lecture about taking care where they walked.

By the time we reached our destination and decided to turn back, sea debris covered the shoreline. Now, my gait is twice as fast as most people (a trait my family always gets after me about). That day I must have been deep in thought, pondering the beauty of the evening and how much I loved the ocean, and I was walking rapidly in front of the rest of the family.

Suddenly I realized someone was walking immediately behind me; I could almost feel his breath. I heard the crunch of feet not my own and looked over my shoulder to see one small son stretching his little legs to put his foot in the last footprint I left in the sand. He thought the only way he could be sure to avoid the broken shells, the jelly fish, and the crabs was to step exactly where I had been. As difficult as it was, he somehow made his feet fit inside the footprints I made, step by painful step.

That long-ago experience left a lasting impression on my soul. Walking behind me are four children trying hard to find my footprints so they can put their feet exactly where their father's have gone.

That's what being a Christian parent is all about. That's why it's such an awesome thing. And that's why we often find ourselves on our face saying, "God, who is sufficient for these things? Lord, help me not to be phony. Help me to embrace Your Word. But most of all, help me to live it. Help me to be the kind of parent who will infect my children with the desire to please You because that's what they see being lived out in my life."

---

1 Ann Landers, *The Dallas Morning News*, March 21, 1991, 2C.

2 V.B. Carter, *Winston Churchill As I Knew Him* (London: Evre, Stotheswoode, and Collins, 1965), 27–28.

3 Carol Kent, *Mothers Have Angel Wings* (Colorado Springs: NavPress, 1997), 33–36.

4 Author unknown.

5 Kent, 57.

6 Josh McDowell, "A Kid's Greatest Hero," *Worldwide Challenge*, May/June 1989, 35.

7 Ibid.

8 Bill Gillham, *Lifetime Guarantee* (Eugene, Ore.: Harvest House Publishers, 1993), n.p.

9 Kent, 74–76.

10 Ann Landers, *The San Diego Union-Tribune*, September 9, 1994.

11 Jean Fleming, *A Mother's Heart* (Colorado Springs: NavPress, 1996), 131

12 Author unknown.

13 Charles R. Swindoll, *You and Your Child: Bible Study Guide* (Fullerton, Calif: Insight for Living, 1986), 5.

Eight

A Home on a Hill

"He commanded our forefathers to teach their children,

so the next generation would ... put their trust in God

and would not forget his deeds but would keep his commands."

—PSALM 78:5-7 (NIV)

*H*ave you ever looked out the window of a plane on a late–night flight? Sometimes I do that (especially when I can't sleep).

Maybe I'll be flying home from a ministry trip, weary and homesick. And the jet will be passing over a some vast expanse of farmland or rangeland–a great sheet of unrelieved black. You may see a little lake or stream, a glint of silver in the moonlight. But most of the time it's just a wide swath of darkness, stretching mile after mile.

And then you see one little, twinkling light.

Immediately, you focus all your attention on that tiny pinprick of yellowish–white. Most likely, it's some lonely farmhouse, far away from any town or main road.

You find yourself wondering about the people dwelling within that little pool of light. Are they up late, reading or watching television? Are they perhaps praying to the Lord at that very moment? Do they have any concept that someone forty thousand feet above them has seen their little light, and is thinking about them?

Jesus said that His disciples are the light of the world. We're to be like cities on hills, visible at a great distance. Especially in the night. As the darkness gathers, the light shines brighter and brighter. It's like a magnet in the gloom…attracting attention…sparking curiosity…drawing people toward the comfort and security and beauty it offers.

I think that's a good picture of the Christian home in today's culture. I believe that one of God's most important tools for extending His kingdom is the Christian family, yours and mine. Did you know God has provided Christian homes for the perpetuation of the faith? He not only wants to use us to bring our children to Christ, but to attract others into a vital relationship with Himself.

Our little family may not be a "city," but we can be a home on a hill, shining in the lonely darkness.

Leading our children to Christ

The Bible says we are to create such an atmosphere in our homes that, at an early age, our children will be drawn to embrace the Lord Jesus

Christ. When we win our children to Christ early, they will be ours and His forever.

I think it's quite impossible for children to grow up in a loving, Christian home in which they receive proper education and example, and not ultimately enjoy the experience of salvation. I frankly don't know any seventeen to nineteen-year-olds who grew up in godly homes who have not come to know Christ as their Savior.

Dr. Harry Ironside, one of the great Bible teachers of the past generation, once wrote:

> I have in my desk, an old, old photograph. It is a photograph of my great-grandfather, just a farmer in Aberdeenshire, Scotland. The photograph is almost faded out with age, though I have tried to keep it covered from the light, because I wanted to have it as long as I might live, for this reason: I have been told many, many times by those who knew my great-grandfather . . . [that] at the close of every day, [he] used to gather all his family . . . about him and have family worship. He always prayed for the salvation and the blessing of his children and his children's children unto the third and fourth generations. . . . As I look at the grizzled face of that old Scottish farmer I thank God for a godly heritage, and I thank Him for the way in which He has answered prayer.[1]

> *"I go to preach with two propositions in mind. First, every person ought to give his life to Christ. Second, whether or not anyone else gives him his life, I will give him mine."*
>
> **—Jonathan Edwards**

Jorie Kinkaid, author of *The Power of Modeling*, wrote that she and her husband "wanted to begin preparing for our children's spiritual births as early as possible, even during pregnancy. Our prayer during each of my pregnancies was for a healthy baby who would come to know Jesus personally, at the earliest age possible. God has answered that prayer in each of our three oldest children's lives, and we continue to pray for our baby."[2]

A faith that spans generations

What kind of faith gets transferred from one generation to another, from godly parent to godly children to godly parent to godly children? If our faith is to live on after we die, it must exhibit some necessary characteristics.

The family of Timothy, the Apostle Paul's protégé, exhibited four of the most important of those characteristics as revealed in 2 Timothy 1:5:

> I call to remembrance the genuine faith that is in you, that dwelt first in your grandmother Lois and your mother Eunice, and I am persuaded is in you also.

According to Acts 16:1, Timothy's mother was a godly Jewess and a believer in Christ. His father was neither. Timothy came from a divided home; his mother was a Christian but his father was not. As a result, Timothy's early spiritual training came from two pious women, his mother Eunice and his grandmother Lois. They taught Timothy the Word of God from his earliest days.

As Timothy watched his mother and grandmother, he saw a consistent example that supported the Bible education he had received. The result was that at an early age he embraced their faith and became "wise for salvation" (2 Timothy 3:15).

What an encouragement this ancient family can be to us! Here is the story of a faith so strong it blossomed through three generations. What kind of faith thrives from generation to generation? I believe it exhibits at least four crucial characteristics.

1. It must be a convincing faith.

Paul said Timothy's "genuine" faith came from his mother and grandmother. The Greek word translated "genuine" is found six times in the New Testament. James 3:17 renders the word "without hypocrisy."

Such a genuine faith is real and convincing.

It goes down deep.

It's not just what we talk about or how we live on Sunday, but touches our lives in every dimension.

If our faith is to blossom in the hearts of our children and children's children after we're gone, it had better be real and authentic and without hypocrisy. If we are to pass on our faith to our children, we must do so along the lines suggested by Deuteronomy 6:6-9. That passage doesn't emphasize formal evangelism techniques as much as how we live in front of our children. *The New International Version* puts it like this:

> These commandments that I give you today are to be upon your hearts. Impress them on your children. Talk about them when you sit at home and when you walk along the road, when you lie down and when you get up. Tie them as symbols on your hands and bind them on your foreheads. Write them on the doorframes of your houses and on your gates.

What we believe must work its way out in the warp and woof of our life. It should be revealed in the total structure and fabric of everything we are.

As I look back on my early days growing up in a Christian family, I realize it wasn't the structured times that most impacted my life. Rather, it was seeing my mother leave her bedroom, tears streaming down her face, as she prayed for each of her children. Sometimes you could hear her praying through the door. What an impression that left on me! She prayed for us every day; it was part of her schedule.

My father, too, taught me much about genuine faith. As the president of a small college, he taught me how to endure intense pressure. When there wasn't enough money to go around and it was difficult to see how we were going to make ends meet, I saw my dad weather the storms, resolute with patience and fairness and love.

I learned more from watching my parents than I ever could have through a formal, structured time of instruction. I gained my lasting values not from daily devotions, but from recognizing love in action and glimpsing the flow of God's Spirit in the everyday routine of living in a Christian home.

No, my parents weren't perfect.

My father was an extremely busy man. Probably too busy. But a "genuine faith" doesn't need to be perfect! Sometimes I saw the reality of their faith when they blew it big-time but faced up to it: "Hey, I really messed up. But God is a God of grace and forgiveness, and will you please pray with me that God will help me not to do this anymore?"

That really impressed me. Here were imperfect people, just like me, willing to admit their shortcomings, leaning hard on Jesus Christ for grace. That's real, authentic faith. I knew my parents loved God with all of their hearts because it translated into the way they lived. That's how I caught their faith. A little poem describes this dynamic better than I can:

> I saw you stand bravely through the years,
> And saw no sign of senseless fears.
> I saw you stand quietly through the stress,
> And saw no glimpse of bitterness.
> I saw you stand prayerfully in grief,
> And saw no sign of unbelief.
> Though you spoke well of Jesus Christ,
> I caught your faith, by watching your life.[3]

If we're to see that kind of faith translated to the next generation, we must pray that God would give it to us first. The genuineness of our walk with God, in all kinds of weather, will be the deciding factor. That will make all the difference in determining whether our faith has staying power.

"We need to model a thirst for Jesus," writes Jorie Kinkaid. "Everyone longs for bright sunshiny days that warm our hearts and make us happy. Our relationship with Jesus may make our children long for a relationship with Him. To me, this element is the key to leading our children to Christ. If I ram religion down my children's throats, I'll likely have rebellious children down the road. Or, I can model such an attractive relationship of my own with Christ that my children may be eager for one, too."[4]

2. It must be a consistent faith.

Paul said that Timothy's genuine faith first "dwelt" in his grandmother Lois and in his mother Eunice. The word "dwelt" means to abide, to live; it has staying power and permanence.

Paul loved to use the word "dwell" when he describes what it means to be a Christian. In 2 Corinthians 6:16 he says, "For you are the temple of the living God. As God has said: 'I will *dwell* in them.'" In 2 Timothy 1:14 he writes, "That good thing which was committed unto you, keep by the Holy Spirit who *dwells* in us." In Colossians 3:16 he says, "Let the Word of Christ *dwell* in you richly."

This metaphor pictures a house with somebody living in it. Christians are like a building whose inhabitant is faith. If our faith is going to be contagious, if our children are going to catch what we have, they must see that our faith is permanent, that it makes it through every crisis that blows into our lives.

Our children learn a whole lot more about our faith from the bad times than they do from the good ones. As our kids sit back and watch us when the troubles come, they're trying to figure out whether we have a lasting faith. They want to know whether this thing we talk about so much really works. Sometimes if we're not careful, we allow our faith to come and go instead of allowing it to dwell in us.

Paul said of Eunice and of Lois that their faith *dwelt* in them. It inhabited their lives, regardless of the circumstances. Because Jesus Christ is the same yesterday, today, and forever, we too can demonstrate His indwelling presence throughout all of life's challenges.

3. It must be a contagious faith.

William Barclay once wrote, "A Christian is a man lost in wonder, love, and praise, at what God has done for him, and aflame with passion to tell others what God can do for them."[5]

Certainly Lois and Eunice had such a passion. They took Timothy under their tutelage and from his earliest days began to teach him the Scriptures. Paul wrote to his young disciple many years later, "Continue in the things you have learned and been assured of, knowing from whom you have learned them, and that from childhood you have known the Holy Scriptures, which are able to make you wise for salvation through faith which is in Christ Jesus" (2 Timothy 3:14–15).

Lois and Eunice couldn't keep quiet about the Lord Jesus. As soon as Timothy was old enough, they started pumping the faith into him. John Calvin says "Timothy was raised in such a way that he could suck in godliness with his mother's milk."[6]

Our faith must be just as contagious. We must be eager to share our faith with our children. Excitement about Jesus Christ conveys a spiritual commitment to our kids that they can never ignore. Author Jorie Kinkaid wisely advises parents to "Keep alert for open doors to speak about Christ...be sensitive to using spontaneous moments to make our children thirsty for God. Don't let opportunities to speak a word for God slip by. If I'm excited about my relationship with Jesus and share that joy with my children, they may want a relationship with Him, too."[7]

By living such a contagious faith, Lois and Eunice reared a godly young man who "was well reported of by the brethren who were at Lystra and Iconium" (Acts 16:2). How did he get that way? Somebody with a contagious faith started to train him when he was a boy and began to mold and shape his character.

Oh, to have such a home! Oh, to be such a mother or father! Oh, to have such an atmosphere for our children! From the moment they come into the world, we can strive to make sure they sense something unique about this place where God has put them.

> *"How hungry and thirsty are you making your children for Jesus Christ? Somebody says, 'You ought to know you can lead a horse to water, but you can't make him drink.' That's right, but you can feed him salt!"*
>
> **—Howard Hendricks**

4. It must be a confident faith.

Paul gave content to his faith at the outset of the passage when he called it "the promise of life which is in Christ Jesus" (2 Timothy 1:1). He called it *the* faith. Paul was talking about absolute faith in Christ, about a life centered in Jesus. Even as a prisoner on his way to death, Paul wrote that the faith in his heart gave him the promise of life. Paul saw life as much more than the beat of his heart within his breast; he saw life as eternal because of his relationship with the eternal Christ.

"Faith" was Paul's ancient watchword, used incessantly in his writings. In Paul's mind, faith meant to embrace Jesus Christ in all of His fullness. Faith was never a mere belief in the head, a bare mental acquiescence to the proof of the historic and dogmatic facts of the Gospel. In the words of Samuel Taylor Coleridge,

"Faith is an affirmation, and an act,
that bids eternal truth be present fact."[8]

Such a confident faith is the only kind we can pass on contagiously. If we're not sure of what we believe, how are we going to make anyone else certain? If we don't know that we have it, how are we going to pass it on to someone else?

Parents, project yourself into the future. Think down through the years–past your children to your grandchildren. What do you see? Will your faith survive your children? Is your faith convincing, consistent, contagious, and confident? If it is, then you have the opportunity to pass on that precious faith to your kids, and they in turn will pass it on to their children.

A classic illustration shows the importance of passing on our faith to the next generation. In a book published a century ago, evangelist D.L. Moody told of two fathers who both lost their sons. But one lost more than the other:

> Whenever I speak to parents, two fathers come before me. One lived on the Mississippi River. He was a man of great wealth. One day his eldest boy had been borne home unconscious. They did everything that man could do to restore him, but in vain. Time passed, and after a terrible suspense he recovered consciousness.
>
> "My son," the father whispered, "the doctor tells me you are dying."
>
> "Oh!" said the boy, "you never prayed for me, Father; won't you pray for my lost soul now?"
>
> The father wept. It was true he had never prayed. He was a stranger to God. And in a little while that soul, unprayed for, passed into its dark eternity.
>
> The father has since said that he would give all his wealth if he could call back his boy only to offer one short prayer for him.
>
> What a contrast to the other father! He, too, had a lovely son, and one day he came home to find him at

the gates of death. His wife was weeping, and she said: "Our boy is dying; he has seen a change for the worse. I wish you would go in and see him."

The father went into the room and placed his hand upon the brow of his dying boy, and could feel the cold, damp sweat was gathering there; the cold, icy hand of death was feeling for the chords of life.

"Do you know, my son, that you are dying?" asked the father.

"Am I? Is this death? Do you really think I am dying?"

"Yes, my son, your end on earth is near."

"And will I be with Jesus tonight, Father?"

"Yes, you will soon be with the Savior."

"Father, don't weep, for when I get there I will go straight to Jesus and tell Him that you have been trying all my life to lead me to Him."[9]

It is our great privilege to lead our children to Christ. By the way we live and by what we say-and through our prayers!-let's allow the beauty of the Savior to shine through with a brilliance that cannot but captivate our children's hearts.

Use your family as an evangelistic tool

God wants to use our homes not only to lead our children to a living faith in Jesus Christ, but also to bring the Gospel to neighbors and friends who don't yet know Him.

Like cities on a hill.

Like a beacon on the block.

Like a lamp in the cul-de-sac.

When observers see how Christ makes a difference under our roofs, they'll want to know what makes us tick. And that's when the glory of Jesus can come blazing through! This is the idea behind 1 Peter 3:15-16 (NIV):

> But in your hearts set apart Christ as Lord. Always be prepared to give an answer to everyone who asks you to

give the reason for the hope that you have. But do this with gentleness and respect, keeping a clear conscience, so that those who speak maliciously against your good behavior in Christ may be ashamed of their slander.

Note that Peter began his instruction by exhorting believers to "set apart Christ as Lord." I like to think of it as building a little sanctuary in our hearts, putting Jesus Christ on the throne there and knowing we have a place to which we may retreat, no matter how severe the storms. Then out of that enthronement flows a readiness to explain the nature of the hope we have. Christ is in control!

It's also telling that Peter did not say, "give an answer for the *faith* that is in you," but "for the *hope* that is in you."

Hope is what shines through to others in times of trouble.

Hope is the inner strength they glimpse in us when the pressure's on.

Hope is the dimension of life they simply can't comprehend.

Viktor Frankl, the Viennese psychiatrist who spent several years in the death camp at Auschwitz, once wrote about hope:

> Any attempt to restore a man's inner strength in the prison camp had first to succeed in showing him some future goal. He who has a "why" to live, can bear almost any "how." Whenever there was an opportunity for it, one had to give them a "why," an aim for their lives in order to strengthen them to bear the terrible "how" of their existence. Woe to him who saw no more sense in his life, no aim, no purpose, and therefore no point in carrying on....Suffering ceases to be suffering in some way at the moment it finds a meaning.[10]

We can get through anything, no matter how hard or difficult, if we know our purpose and goal and future and hope. The result of losing all hope is the loss of desire to live. When people lose all hope, they jump off bridges, blow their brains out, overdose on pills, and end their lives.

But a hope burning within us will take us through even the most difficult circumstances. Peter said when folks see that hope in us, they will come to us and say, "Why are you so hopeful with all these terrible things happening? I know you're going through difficult times, but you still have a smile on your face and a sense of peace in your heart. Listen, I've never seen anybody like you. Why is it that you are the way you are?"

When that happens, Peter said, "Be ready always to give them an answer." The word "answer" is the Greek *apologia*, a defense. We need to be able to give a defense for our hope.

And how do we do that? Not in arrogance. We aren't to get up on our soapbox and let them have it. The point is never to let them know how smart we are or how skilled we might be at defending our faith. We are to give them a reason for our hope "with meekness and fear, having a good conscience."

Meekness is power under control; it's strength gone underground. When someone asks us why we are the way we are, with a gentle and quiet spirit we respond—not with a desire to win an argument, but with a longing to win over the spirit of the inquisitor. We are to answer with meekness, reverence, and out of a good conscience.

And when we do this—when we go in knowing that we're walking with the Lord, that we're prepared to meet the challenge, when we have a quiet, meek spirit, the truth of God's Word, and a clean life—we're the most powerful tool in God's arsenal. There is nothing like the force of a clear conscience in doing warfare for God!

Joe Aldrich, the former president of Multnomah Bible College, can heartily testify to the truth of this principle. In the book *Gentle Persuasion* he describes an encounter with a long-lost neighbor:

> I was speaking in Colorado on "Cultivating, Sowing, and Reaping: The Three Phases of Evangelism." After the service, a young woman approached and asked, "Joe,

"We become God's living work of art in the world by putting ourselves in the way of his light and letting him shine through us. If we want to be windows of God's light to the other members of our family, we must put ourselves in the light's way and stay there."

—**Karen Mains**

do you remember me?"

I didn't. I told the truth.

"Well, I used to baby-sit for your son."

Oh, that's right. But that was ten years ago! How would she expect me to remember?

"I want you to know that two years ago someone shared Christ with me, and I became a believer. But the reason I trusted Christ was because of what I saw ten or fifteen years ago."

"What you saw ten years ago?"

"Yes! When I used to walk across the green strip of grass between your house and mine, it was like going from darkness to light. I couldn't figure out what made your home and family so different from mine."

"You're kidding!" I said.

"No, I'm serious. After I put your kids to bed, I used to go into the den and pull books off the shelf to try to find out what made you tick. When I'd leave your house to return home, it was like going from light back to darkness again."

Then she asked a very perceptive question.

"Is that why you used to wax my dad's car?"

Her dad loved automobiles, but couldn't do much to maintain them because of a heart condition. I'd learned that if you love what somebody else loves, you'll be loved. That's just what happened.

I'd ask her father to give me his car keys, then I'd wash and wax his auto. He'd pull up a folding chair and we'd talk and talk. Not about spiritual things. He wasn't ready. His family was part of our neighborhood network, and we did lots of things together.

I'm delighted to report that the gospel has gone down through webs of relationships into that family unit. It started with a can of wax, a listening ear, and a curious baby-sitter. My prayer is that the entire *oikos* will be saved.[11]

What's an *"oikos"*? you might be wondering. *Oikos* is a Greek word that means "household." Joe defines an *oikos* as "a social system built around family and friends,"[12] and he insists that the most effective evangelism occurs among these webs of relationships. In other words, your household can be an effective tool to bring other households to Christ!

Joe closes his chapter on "Cashing In on Your Networks" by writing, "'Charity begins at home,' an old saying goes. I'm not sure I like the idea, but it might grow on me if you changed the first word to 'Evangelism.' *Evangelism* begins at home...especially in your 'home neighborhood.' Which *oikos* in yours looks ready?"[13]

To readers who feared their *"oikos* potential" seemed limited because they hadn't yet flowed into the homes, lives, and experiences of many non-Christians, Joe had some advice. Why not get involved in a garden club, a Pop Warner football league, a neighborhood association, the PTA, a trade association, a service club, or with the parents of your children's friends?

Joe went on: "Ruthe and I have thoroughly enjoyed our kids' friends. They are a delight to have around. We consider them our own. Nearly every vacation, we take along someone else's teenager. Try sending these kids with your child to a good Christian camp. It's a great way to reach a family! Make your kids' friends feel welcome. Go out of your way to befriend them. Make an effort to become acquainted with their parents. If the teenagers like you, their parents will know it. And vice versa."[14]

Joe Aldrich, of course, is only one of millions who have learned the joy of using their *oikos* to reach out to neighbors and friends who don't yet know Christ. Pastor Calvin Ratz tells of a friend named Tom who has learned the same lesson:

> Tom is a mechanic who came to the Lord a couple of years ago. Many of his friends continue to drop by to talk about old times. One of his friends, a truck driver named Gord, was an introvert. He had no personal church experience, but he did have strong opinions about preachers and what he *thought* went on in church. The idea of conversing with a preacher turned him off.
>
> However, Gord was intrigued by the change in Tom

and started asking questions. Tom told Gord what had happened to him and how he could experience the same thing. Gord and his wife eventually came to the church with Tom's family, and then Tom brought them to see me. We talked for a couple of hours, setting them at ease and sharing the way of salvation. The next week we met again, and Gord and his wife each committed themselves to Christ. The final decision was made in my office, but it was Tom who had brought them to a place of faith.

Tom's friends were not afraid or intimidated by him. He was unencumbered by the negative images outsiders have of preachers and the church. In addition, he had just experienced a radical change in his life that was noticed by non-Christians. It's the Toms in our churches who are the keys to evangelism, and growing churches are committed to helping their Toms reach their friends for Christ.[15]

Free-lance writer M. Thomas Russell joined his voice to the chorus when he wrote, "A former pastor of mine says that before his conversion, he regularly crossed paths with a consistent Christian. He resisted his witness for years, but eventually yielded. 'He simply outlived me,' my pastor friend says. Over time, the other man's words and faith were more than a match for a stubborn unbeliever.

"Many a Christian tells the same story. It usually takes years of sowing and watering and nurturing to produce a crop . . . people who daily plug away in the fields, demonstrating biblical principles among unbelievers, outliving them until a reaper gathers the harvest. The Bible acknowledges the teamwork: 'The man who plants and the man who waters have one purpose, and each will be rewarded according to his own labor' (1 Corinthians 3:8)."[16]

These testimonies, and thousands of others like them, demonstrate that God wants to use our homes and families to reach others with the Gospel. And I do mean "families"-not just Mom and Dad! Our children, too, can know the joy of becoming a mighty tool in the hand of God for bringing friends to Christ.

The powerful testimony of abstinence

God can use our children in untold creative ways to introduce others to the Savior, but let me briefly describe just one effective means. Do our kids realize that sexual abstinence until marriage is a powerful testimony to a watching world? First Thessalonians 4:5 says we are to conduct ourselves as Christians, "Not in passion of lust, like the Gentiles who do not know God."

When Christians live a promiscuous life, they're living just like the world, out of which they were called. Why should pagans adhere to high moral standards? They don't know God–but we do. That means we should be different.

We should encourage our children that they can be proud to be like NBA stars A.C. Green or David Robinson, who have made outspoken stands for sexual purity. We can teach our sons and daughters to stand up among their peers and say, "Go ahead, guys, if you want to do that. Play your Russian roulette. But I have made a commitment to Christ and I am not ashamed to keep that commitment until marriage."

> *"Every child brought into this world can make a significant contribution. Christian homes are the salt of the earth. But if we stop producing salt, what will happen to our influence?"*
>
> **—Steve Farrar**

Some years ago the friends of a teenage girl were badgering her because she was supposedly the only virgin in their group. Every time she'd get together for a party with her friends, they'd ask her if she had yet gone "all the way." This girl was a Christian and struggled how to respond. Finally one day she gave an answer that put an end to all their pressure. "Anytime I want I can be just like you are," she declared. "But you can never again be like I am."

Wow! You might want to write that one down; it's worth having in your kids' arsenal of answers. Just for the record, I've also heard the following answers our young people can give when others are pressuring them to go to bed:

"Everybody's doing it."

Well then, you should have no problem finding somebody else to do it with.

"I want to show my love to you in a real way."

OK, buy me a ring, size 5, no less than two carats.

"It's my hormones. I just can't help myself."

Oh yeah? I'll bet if my six-foot seven daddy was sitting in the back seat, you'd be able to help yourself.

"Come on, baby, if you love me you'll let me."

No, if you loved me, you wouldn't ask.

"It's only natural."

So is diarrhea, but I wouldn't want to participate in it on a daily basis. If you cannot control your bodily functions by age fifteen, we need to check you into a hospital; there's something wrong. I've never read an obituary that says, "Johnny died of virginity."[17]

No doubt some kids will mock our children for deciding to remain virgins until marriage, but others will notice their firm stance and will wonder, *How can they be so strong? I'd like to be able to follow their lead, but it's too tough. I can't take the abuse. What do they have that I don't?*

The answer, of course, is Jesus. More than one young person will be in heaven someday because of a Christian friend who chose to remain sexually pure, whatever the cost!

No one's too young

God wants to use our families to bring others into the family of God and He is an expert at using every kind of household tool imaginable-Mom, Dad, older brother, and even little sister. As parents, we have the priceless opportunity to let our kids know how they can fit into the eternal plans of God. No one is too small or too young to be used by God to introduce others to Jesus.

I won't belabor the point. But do allow me to tell a single story that highlights the place even our youngest can have in the work of evangelism. This tale comes from a time past, but continues to illustrate how God longs to use each of us in spreading the Good News.

When Evelyn McClusky was six years old, her father, a pastor, invited evangelist R.A. Torrey to Texarkana for city-wide tent meetings. Evelyn took a handful of cards announcing the meetings and began passing them out in her neighborhood. Whenever she'd give someone a card, she'd also recite a Bible verse.

She writes:

> For several days I was welcomed with a smile at every house. Then I remembered that new neighbors had

moved in about a block away. I found their house behind a white picket fence, its gate latched.

I lifted the little iron bar. The gate groaned and squeaked. A massive dog behind the house barked and ran toward me. I was not afraid of a dog! "Nice doggie," I said, and proceeded to the door.

As I stepped on the porch, a man opened the door and asked kindly, "What do you want, little girl?"

I extended a card and said, "I brought you an invitation to the tent meeting."

By the time I had reached this house, I was running short of memorized verses. But I hurriedly reached in my mind and came up with, "And after this the judgment."

"It's in Hebrews 9, but I have forgotten the verse number," I explained.

The man scowled at me, handed the card back, and said, "I'm not interested in the tent meeting. Go away!"

I ran for the gate. Then I paused and thought, *That man doesn't love Jesus. I gave him the wrong verse.* Trembling, I returned and knocked on his door again. I gave him another card and said, "I'm sorry I gave you that verse. Here is a better one. 'For God so loved the world that He gave...'".

Before I could complete the verse, he angrily tore the card, threw it at me, and yelled, "Don't come back!"

My eyes filled with tears as I made my way back to the squeaky gate. When I lifted the latch, I turned back and saw the man standing, red-faced, at his door. I waved and called to him, "I'll be praying for you." Tears dropped as I went home to tell Mother what had happened.

On the morning of the tent meeting, Mother took me to the dry goods store to select a dress pattern. She was trying to console me, knowing that I had been praying for the unfriendly neighbor for a week. "Do you need to measure me, Mother?" I asked. "If not, may

I go next door and give out these two last cards to the tent meeting?"

"Yes, but make it quick. The meetings begin tonight."

I trotted to the nearby music store, handed one of the cards to the young lady in charge of the sheet music department, and recited a verse. "How sweet," she said, smiling.

Then I turned to the young man in the horn department. "How bright your horns are," I said, handing him an invitation. I had just started to quote a verse when a man stepped from behind a partition dividing the store. It was the new neighbor I had wept over for a week!

"And stay away from *here*, too!" he stormed.

I hurried back to Mother. In her arms I sobbed, "The man I'm praying for is next door."

That evening, crowds of people streamed into the big tent. The fresh sawdust scented the air as Dr. Torrey's hefty assistant, with arms flailing, led the singing. My father sat beside Dr. Torrey. Mother was in the choir. I was in the center of the tent, sitting on a new bench beside Miss Ann.

After Dr. Torrey had finished his sermon, we started singing again. People were walking forward to accept Jesus as their Savior. Suddenly, the song leader stopped the singing and called out, "A man has come forward who wants to know if there is a little girl in the audience who has been giving out invitations to the meetings. She has brown hair."

I patted Miss Ann's arm and eagerly whispered, "May I stand up on the bench? I want to see the other little girl who has been giving out invitations."

Before Miss Ann could stop me, I was on the bench straining to see. Then I saw the man I had been praying for!

Suddenly the man pointed to me and exclaimed, "There she is!" He extended his arms and said, "Come, child." I scattered sawdust running to him.

He hurried down the steps, bent one knee in the sawdust, and bent the other knee to make a seat for me. He held me close and dropped tears on my brown hair, which was caught on his vest button. I did not wince when it pulled, because I was too caught up in his happy words.

"Child, I couldn't get away from your prayers and God's verse, especially 'After this the judgment.' I've come to Jesus. He is my Savior."[18]

God is so big that no one is too little to bring the Good News of Jesus Christ to those who don't yet know Him. Through the power of Almighty God, our families can become bastions of light and life to our neighbors who sorely lack both.

Train them to reach out to ever wider circles
God wants to use our homes, first to reach our children for Christ, then to reach out to our neighbors and friends. But our households can reach even beyond that. Some of the happiest homes I know are households in which a concern for the whole world is both taught and caught.

Did you know that, according to Ralph Winter (founder of the U.S. Center for World Mission), *80 percent* of today's missionaries caught the vision when they were children? And where did they catch it? At home!

Noel Piper is the wife of John Piper, pastor of missions-minded Bethlehem Baptist Church in Minneapolis, Minnesota. Several years ago she wrote an article titled "Home-Grown World Christians" in which she declared, "Our most basic prayer for our children is that God will move them toward Himself. That they will be His people. That they will become men of God. And then our prayer is that, as they focus on God, they will be aware of the world that needs Him too."[19]

Noel suggested that parents consciously expose their kids to other children and families who are different culturally from them. She recommended that parents introduce their children to international students, to Asian emigrants, to American Indians and migrant farm workers and people of color. "Continuous contact with people of other cultures and circumstances prepares our children to be open to and comfortable with people anywhere," she wrote. "We assume aloud that many people don't know God. In every place we've lived-suburbs or city-our children have had playmates with unmarried parents living together. They have learned early that many people don't go to church and many get drunk and smear God's name with filth. And those are just the outward signs of what's inside even more people. And, we tell them, if people close to us are living without God, just think how much worse it is in places where no teachers of Jesus have come and where there are no churches?"[20]

Missionaries flow in and out of the Piper home, just as other friends do. Missionaries Harvey and Barbara Esplund once were moved to tears when Abraham Piper, then four years old, ran up to them and said, "I know you. You're the Esplunds from the Philippines." He had never met the couple, but he recognized them through the Piper's family prayers and because he loved to look at the pictures in the *Daily Prayer Calendar.*[21]

So how can we rear kids who become "world Christians"? Noel offered several suggestions: Read *National Geographic;* read aloud missionary biographies and stories with foreign settings; include our children in conversations with foreign students, missionaries, and emigrants; go to the airport to send off missionary friends; use the Internet to look up geographical and religious information on foreign countries.

From their earliest days, our children can learn that God loves the whole world-and that they can have a part in bringing others to a saving knowledge of Jesus Christ, whether those people live under their own roof, in their own neighborhood, or on the other side of the world. God is a big God, and He wants to use *them* in His global plans to display His glory among the nations.

Bottom line: Get to Jesus!

Psalm 78:5-7 (NIV) says God "commanded our forefathers to teach their children, so the next generation would...put their trust in God and would not forget his deeds but would keep his commands."

That's one job description that never yellows with age. It's as fresh and relevant today as it was when it was penned millennia ago.

One of our biggest and most delightful jobs as parents is to lead our children to Christ, then to help them find their own place in God's worldwide work of evangelism. The methods we use and the opportunities God gives us may be almost without number, but one thing remains the same through everything. I'll let Woodie White name it:

> In the fall of 1953 I met a young woman at a soda fountain. At the time I was having severe difficulty with organized religion. She was an articulate and dedicated Christian. She knew how to talk about her faith. The more I railed against the church, the more she talked about Jesus. The more I talked about the hypocrites in the church, the more she talked about Jesus. The more I pointed to the failure of the church, the more she talked about Jesus. She won. Praise God!
>
> Maybe we are using our evangelistic witness to talk about the wrong things. Perhaps we are giving answers to questions no one is asking. It may well be that people are looking for bread and we are giving a stone. The Good News is: Jesus is Lord! Whatever else may follow, and there is much, this is where the Story begins.[22]

This is the Story which can energize us and our children to partner with God in the most exciting work in the world. The Lord of the universe wants to use *us* in the proclamation of the most important message the world will ever receive! Let's respond with joy to that call, and let's ask God to use our families to help others discover what we already know:

Jesus is Lord!

1 H.A. Ironside, *Timothy, Titus and Philemon* (Neptune, N.J.: Loizeaux Brothers, 1976), 163.

2 Jorie Kinkaid, *The Power of Modeling* (Colorado Springs: NavPress, 1989), 138–139.

3 Author unknown.

4 Kinkaid, 141.

5 William Barclay, *The Letters to Timothy, Titus, and Philemon* (Philadelphia: The Westminster Press, 1975), 142.

6 John Calvin, *The Epistles of Paul to Timothy and Titus, 1548* (Oliver and Boyd, 1964), 292.

7 Kinkaid, 142.

8 Guy H. King, *To My Son: An Expositional Study of II Timothy* (Fort Washington, Pa.: Christian Literature Crusade, 1962), 16.

9 D.L. Moody, *Moody's Anecdotes, Incidents and Illustrations* (Chicago: The Bible Institute Culportage Association, 1898), 22–23.

10 Viktor Frankl, *Man's Search for Meaning* (New York: Simon & Schuster, Inc., 1984), 84–85.

11 Joe Aldrich, *Gentle Persuasion* (Portland, Ore.: Multnomah Press, 1988), 141–142.

12 Ibid., 139.

13 Ibid., 146–147.

14 Ibid., 190–191.

15 Calvin Ratz, *Mastering Outreach & Evangelism* (Portland, Ore.: Multnomah Press, 1990), 64.

16 M. Thomas Russell, "They'll Probably Wake Up in the Morning," *Moody,* May 1990, 23.

17 Author unknown.

18 From "Come to the Tent Meeting, Mister," by Evelyn M. McClusky, publication and date unknown.

19 Noel Piper, "Home-Grown World Christians," *The Standard,* March 1989, 10.

20 Ibid., 10–11.

21 Ibid., 12.

22 Woodie W. White, "At the Soda Fountain," *Good News,* Jan/Feb 1986.

When Strings
Turn to Wings

"Children are the living messages

we send to a time that we will not see."

—NEIL POSTMAN

*I*t seems like only yesterday that I hugged and kissed my nineteen-year-old Jennifer just before she stepped onto a USAir 767 taking her back to Dayton, Ohio, and the third quarter of her freshman year at Cedarville College.

Moments later I put my arms around my older son, David, and held him to me for a while before I hugged and kissed his beautiful wife, Cami, and watched them walk off toward the American Airlines corridor and their flight back home to Raleigh, North Carolina.

Seven of us suddenly had become four.

We headed back to San Diego and later that afternoon drove to Coronado, where I dropped off my older daughter, Jan, and hugged and kissed her outside the door to the apartment she then called "home."

And then we were down to three.

For seven straight nights, all seven of us had eaten dinner together at the same table at the same time in the same place. Neither Donna nor I could remember when that had last occurred even when we all lived in the same house. What a memory-making week for the Jeremiah family, a precious, joyous gift of one whole week spent with those who are the dearest to us on this earth!

In many ways, it seemed as if we had never been apart. I think it's like that for families who are close. There is no period of adjustment, no getting used to each other. It's as if we picked up the conversations where we last left them. But by Saturday the conversations ended and we split three ways to get back to "normal."

Did I say "normal"?

That was normal then; these days our home is down to two. Daniel, our youngest, is now a sophomore at Appalachian State University, clear across a wide continent in Boone, North Carolina. And Donna and I feel the empty-nest syndrome in full force.

It doesn't seem fair

As your kids become older, you become aware that you are losing control, little by little. Frankly, that's what parenting is all about...the gradual losing of control. That's when we get our grade card; that's when we find out how well we've done.

Ultimately all of us must say good-bye to our kids.

Yet sometimes I find myself thinking angry thoughts about the process of emptying the nest. It just doesn't seem fair to invest twenty prime years-the best years of your life-in four kids, only to see them walk away one by one and leave you for their own lives.

I mean, whose idea was this, anyway?

Let me answer my own question from Genesis 2:24: "Therefore a man shall leave his father and mother and be joined to his wife, and they shall become one flesh." The Bible makes clear that this whole leaving thing was God's idea. It's easy to get mad at people-but how do you get mad at God?

As sad as we sometimes feel, as much as we grieve, as often as dread sneaks into our lives when our kids move into their high-school years, we need to remember this: the empty nest was God's idea. But more than that. It was God *the Father's* idea.

The same Father-God who spent an eternity in fellowship with His Son, and then, in love for all of us, sent Him away for thirty-three years to this world which cared nothing for Him, dreamed up the idea of kids growing into adults and moving away. God the Father has not asked any earthly father to do anything which He has not already done Himself.

One author put it this way: "Why, Lord, if we do it the way You tell us to do it, sacrificing and pouring our lives into the lives of our children—why does it hurt so much when they go? Is pain the price we pay for doing it Your way?" And the writer continued, "I seem to hear a whisper in my ear: 'Yes, My child, because love does cost. It cost Me My Son.'"[1]

Over the past few years I've begun many discussions with the Father about my feelings over this leaving home business. As I have talked with Him about it-in very passionate tones-I sense He understands my point of view.

I must admit that although Donna and I are nearly through this passageway, we are not experts on how to handle the conflicting emotions that erupt when strings turn to wings. Some people say, "This is going to be a very lonely time." Others exclaim, "My goodness! It's like a second honeymoon." Still others, obviously suffering from some difficult experiences, say, "Change the locks. They keep coming back!" Last, of course, come those who champion grandparenting, who tell you it's the best time of all.

One thing we can know for sure: it *is* a time of change. As C.S. Lewis once wrote, "To live in time is to change because time is change."[2] For me and for many of the people I know, change is tough. It puts us through the wringer. We dread the very thought of it.

Erma Bombeck, writing about the day she put her baby on the bus to kindergarten, said, "My excuse for everything just got on that bus....These walls have been so safe for the last few years. I didn't have to prove anything to anyone. Now I feel vulnerable. What if I apply for a job and no one wants me? What if I can't let go of my past?"[3]

When strings turn to wings, what do we do? How do we prepare for it? I wish there were some passage in the Bible to which we could turn, some unique story of the Scriptures which would contain all the information we need.

But it's not like that.

In fact, leaving home in Bible times didn't happen like it does today. Sons and daughters left to be a part of the extended family; the whole group largely stayed together through most of their lives. Rarely was there any moving across the continent or being far apart as we know it today.

But there are some principles we can glean, and in this chapter I'd like to offer some wisdom based on family experiences, advice we have received from others, and eternal truth from the Word of God.

Begin now to prepare for the empty nest

We have to prepare ourselves for the very natural sense of loss we will feel when our children leave home. Until we start sending our kids off to college, we are often unaware of how much of our time, energy, and emotion has been invested in them.

Then one day, they're gone.

And we are left with a great, aching empty place in the middle of our hearts that we don't know what to do with.

Part of the sadness of our children leaving home is the realization that we are growing older. That's why parents almost universally react upon hearing "Sunrise, Sunset," a bittersweet song from the great musical *Fiddler on the Roof*.

> "At a turning point in his ministry, John the Baptist said of the Lord Jesus, 'He must increase, I must decrease.' That's the role of the parent with our own little home-grown disciples. They must increase; but we must decrease. Their personal responsibility to the Lord must increase; their personal responsibility to Dad and Mom must decrease."
>
> **—Stu Weber**

Jan was the first of ours to leave home. I remember taking her to Schroon Lake, New York, where she was enrolled at Word of Life Bible Institute. We went there together, just the two of us, and stayed in an old cabin by the lake. Everything seemed cold and dark. If you live in California, as I do, you forget how overcast the skies can grow back east. You forget how heavy and leaden that can feel. That day was dreary, dark, and sad, and that night I didn't sleep much.

We got up early the next morning and walked to registration, held in a huge gymnasium loaded with tables festooned with tall signs and manned by total strangers. I asked my daughter, "Do you want me to go through registration with you?"

"I think I can do it myself," she replied. And so she did.

Later we met for lunch. And all too soon it was time for me to go. I climbed in my rental car and drove ninety miles back down the mountain to the Albany airport, silently and alone. I came home without my daughter. I'm not ashamed to admit it was a terribly sad journey.

It was four o'clock in the morning when David left. If you're not going to sleep all night, I suppose you might as well get up at four o'clock. He and David Beezer, his good buddy, packed all their stuff in the back of our David's Ford Ranger truck, threw a tarp over everything and tied it down, then headed off twenty-seven hundred miles to Liberty University in Lynchburg, Virginia, to play football.

And I stood in the driveway at 4 A.M. and sobbed like a baby.

I couldn't stop myself. Eventually I became so weary I walked in the house and sat down in a tired heap. And you know what? My grief didn't evaporate right away. When you send your children away, the sadness hits in the strangest ways and at the oddest times.

I used to jog around a block near David's high school. The first day after David left for college I went running, trying to stay in shape. I did fine until I rounded the corner and jogged down the street. I ran by the stadium where David had played football-and began to weep.

Now understand, I was nearing the end of my five-mile jog. I was panting so hard I could hardly breathe. It's tough to cry when it feels as if all the oxygen in the world has leached into the soil! Yet there I was, breathing hard, the tears rolling down my cheeks, my aching legs still pumping-and I thought, *Should I stop? No! I don't want anybody to see me like this!* So I dragged myself home as quickly as I could.

Even then, the sorrow didn't dissipate for some time. One mother who knows about "the sadness" said it hit her when she went to the grocery store and realized she didn't have to buy her son's favorite breakfast cereal anymore because he wouldn't be there to eat it.[4]

The year Jennifer left for school I took her and her mother to Lindbergh Field to get on a plane. They were going a week early so they could buy winter clothes in a place where such necessities didn't cost as much as they do in San Diego. Donna was going to help her get settled in the dorm and ready for school. So the two of them boarded the plane...and left me standing there, all by myself. I came home and realized that life was really changing for the Jeremiah family. Strings were turning to wings.

All this began to dawn on me back in 1989, the year I read one of the most emotional letters ever to come from the pen of Dr. James Dobson. In that July's letter, Dr. Dobson described his moment of great grief after his second child and only son left home. He wrote:

> There I was, driving down the freeway, when an unexpected wave of grief swept over me. I thought I couldn't stand it to see him go. It's not that I dreaded or didn't look forward to what the future held. No. I mourned the loss of an era, a precious time of my life when our children were young, and their voices rang in the halls

of our home.[5]

Dr. Dobson then described sitting on the floor in his son's room, looking at all the memories it contained, and realizing that though his son would return, things would never be the same. From that moment on, life would be different for the Dobson family.

We must prepare for the empty-nest syndrome, and the first step to take toward that end is to fully realize: it happens. If we are unprepared, our kids' leaving can put us on the defensive very quickly. Preparation is everything.

> "The greatest love we can lavish upon our children is to train them in the fear of God, equip them for life, and then release them."
>
> **—Floyd McClung**

Resume the adventure

We've talked enough about the sadness of the empty-nest syndrome. Now let's consider the other side.

First, it's time to resume the adventure of marriage-without-children-around! A house without kids is not the end of your life; it's merely the end of one chapter in your life. One reason we need to cultivate our relationship with our spouse, even while we're busily rearing our children, is that one of these days the kids will all be gone and we'll be alone once more with our wife or husband. We'd better be friends when that time comes!

After the children are gone, we tend to remember all the wonderful times when they were still home. We somehow forget all the Saturday nights we stayed up late, way past the time they were supposed to be home, waiting for them to walk through the door. It tends to slip our minds how much we worried about where they were, who they were with, what they were doing, and how they were doing it. Rearing kids is a grand adventure, but it has its downsides.

A teacher asked her class what each student wanted to become when he or she grew up. One boy said, "President." Another said, "I want to be a fireman." A third said, "I want to be a teacher." One by one they answered until they came to Billy. When his turn came, the teacher asked, "Billy, what do you want to be when you grow up?"

"I want to be possible," Billy answered.

With a question mark on her face the teacher asked, "What do you mean, you want to be possible?"

"Well," Billy replied, "my mom is always telling me I'm impossible. When I grow up I want to become possible."

Most people tell me that the next chapter in their lives after the kids leave home is even more exciting than what went before. Donna and I were married for six years before we had children. We remember those years with great fondness and excitement. In a word, we were unencumbered. And that meant spontaneity! Did you ever try spontaneity with four little ones at home? There is no such thing. Everything revolves around where they are, what they're doing, who's taking care of them, and "what do we do now?"

Those childless years were wonderful years. We had so much fun together as a couple! We went out to eat when we wanted to go out to eat. We explored new places when we wanted to explore new places. We did whatever we wanted whenever we wanted to do it. It was great. And so we look forward once more to the freedom of such years.

There truly are good things to look forward to when strings turn to wings. The grandest is that we have the joy of refocusing on each other in our marital relationship. We shouldn't be so sad about the loss of our children that we can't refocus on what we still have. Let's not dwell on what is lost, but on what is left. And there's much!

And some new things too!

Once the nest has been empty for some time, usually a husband and wife start noticing other eggs–but this time they're lying in someone else's nest. Namely, your son's or daughter's! And the time for grand-parenting has arrived.

Naomi, the beloved mother–in–law of Ruth in the Old Testament, could not hide her elation when she heard she had become a grandma. After the birth of her grandson Obed, it is said that "Naomi took the child and laid him on her bosom and became a nurse to him" (Ruth 4:16). That is an Old Testament euphemism for expressing the love a grandmother has for her grandson. Naomi became Obed's nurse. What a wonderful picture of the love of a grandmother for her grandchildren!

It's a special thing when a grandmother or grandfather holds their grandchild in their arms. (For one thing, it's special because you can set a limit on how long you have them!) All of us grandparents understand that.

To announce that my first grandson, David Todd Jeremiah, was on his way, David and Cami held a little surprise party for Donna and me. They summoned us home at an unusual time, causing me to think something was wrong. They presented us with two gifts, one for Donna and one for me. The package I opened had something to do with being a grandfather, but I missed its meaning. I just looked at it, mystified.

But the moment Donna opened her gift, she turned instantly from a Baptist into a Charismatic. I have never seen my wife dance in the Lord, but she danced that day! And her excitement has not waned at all in the months since then. David Todd is sixteen months old at this writing, and when I see how much my wife loves him, I am reminded afresh of the wonderful bond that exists between grandparents and their grandchildren.

Being a grandfather is one of the most exciting things in the world. Everywhere I travel I find wonderful shirts for my grandson that brag about his granddad. I buy every one of them. I don't let him wear one particular shirt to church, however–I mean the one that says, "Don't mess with me. My grandfather's the meanest, baddest man in town." (I do like it, though. Maybe he could wear it to school someday.)

Someone has written that a baby has a way of making a man out of his father and a boy out of his grandfather. That's true! Before David Todd came along, it had been a long time since I'd been down on the floor, playing with toys. But I am back to doing that again.

It is no wonder the Bible says Naomi was "blessed." Grandchildren have a way of doing that to grandparents. They're a big reason that the new adventure of empty-nesting can be so fabulous.

Arrows to our rescue

A verse we considered at the beginning of this book also has an important place at the end. Psalm 127:3-5 says:

> Behold, children are a heritage from the Lord,
> The fruit of the womb is a reward.
> Like arrows in the hand of a warrior,

So are the children of one's youth.
Happy is the man who has his quiver full of them.
They shall not be ashamed,
But shall speak with their enemies in the gate.

The psalmist says our children are like arrows. And what does an arrow do? It goes to a place we can't go, to accomplish a purpose we can't accomplish. Isn't it incredible to see how God raises up our children and thrusts them out into the world to do His work? And think about this: whatever good your children do, wherever they are, a part of *you* is doing whatever they're doing. You are in them; your life has been built into their life. They're an arrow shot from your bow to do good for God.

But not only that. This text insists that when our children are grown, we will not be ashamed, for they shall speak with our enemies in the gate. What does this mean? It's a wonderful picture of what happened in Solomon's day.

In those days all business was transacted at the city gate and all major disputes were decided there. Solomon means that if we rear godly children, when we get older and land in trouble, they will come and stand with us, helping us out and speaking up for us. That's why we won't need to be ashamed.

As we grow older, it's good to know we have some kids out there who will come and stand with us and encourage us. Some of us are in that process with our own parents right now–and it won't be too many years before our own children will be in that process with us. God has raised us up to stand with our parents in a time when they really need our help, and He is doing the same thing with our own kids.

> *"Millennia ago, the invention of the bow and arrow changed the face of warfare forever. For the first time, a warrior could impact a battle scene from a great distance. Similarly, our children are the only messages we'll send to a world we'll never see. They are the only provision we have for impacting a world at a distance."*
>
> **—Stu Weber**

Take the initiative to stay close

I've heard all the stories about how a grown son never calls home or a faraway daughter never writes, how parents send postage stamps to their kids so that their chances of hearing some news might slightly increase. I know all of that, but I've concluded that it is we parents who must take the initiative to keep the family close when our kids live far away. It's our job. And we need to do so without interference or intervention.

When David played high-school football, I was such an avid fan that it almost killed me to think he was leaving home to attend a college where I couldn't often see him play. So I bought a satellite dish, hoping to find a few stray broadcasts. No such luck. So in his first year at Liberty University, I flew across the country to attend five of his football games. I'd preach on Thursday or Friday somewhere in the Lynchburg area, then watch the game on Saturday. Only my wife knows how many times I almost didn't make it back to San Diego for Sunday services.

And now, my second son, Daniel, is playing quarterback for Appalachian State University in Boone, North Carolina. It seems like they keep going farther and farther away! Even though Donna and I are a few years older than we were when we chased David around, still we have managed to see all of Daniel's games. When he recently scored the winning touchdown in an upset win over Wake Forest University, I hugged his mother and said, "Aren't you glad we were here for this important moment?"

Personal visits are the best, but the phone is a wonderful tool to keep the family close when our kids live far away. One lady in our church told me she gave phone cards to her three adult children and told them they could use the cards anytime to call home or to call their siblings. Never once did they abuse the privilege. The system kept the family close when the kids lived far away.

These days there's yet another gift from heaven that helps families stay in touch. It's called e-mail. At Cedarville College Jennifer had a computer in her room, as all students did. Quickly she was into e-mail. When her mother heard about it, she got e-mail on her computer too. David and Daniel soon followed suit. Today all of them send letters back and forth. When Donna and I return home after we've been away, she immediately heads to the back room where the computer sits.

The first time she did this I asked, "Where are you going?" She replied, "I'm going to see if I have any mail," turned on the computer, and searched for new messages. I just looked on, speechless.

One time Jennifer called from Cedarville to say she was doing an assignment and needed some research help. I have a great library, so I told her I'd be glad to find what she needed. When I called back a little later to give her the required information, I said, "Are you ready?"

"What do you mean?" she asked.

"I'm going to read this little paragraph to you over the phone," I replied.

She *laughed* at me!

"Daddy, why are you going to do that? Give it to Mom. She'll type it in e-mail and it'll come right out on the paper." Oh, the wonders of e-mail!

As I think of my dearly loved sons and daughters, it is my hope that Donna and I will always take the initiative to keep our family close. Our family is too precious for us to allow our hard-earned closeness to slip away.

Plan for your children to return

Of course, just because our kids leave our home, doesn't mean they'll never return. And I don't mean just at Christmas and for vacation times.

A brand new thing in our culture developed during the time you and I have been adults. Adult children are returning home, not just to visit, but to *move in*. Some have called them "boomerang kids." Data from a recent survey says that of midlife parents aged forty-five to fifty-four who have adult children, forty-five percent have an adult child living at home.[6]

Several acronyms have been created to describe this new phenomenon. One is RYAS, Returning Young Adult Syndrome. The other is ILYA, Incompletely Launched Young Adults.[7]

A lot of people have asked me, "Pastor, what do you do when your adult child wants to move back home?" The first thing to do is to ask how long you and your spouse have to make your decision. Then you talk to your spouse and pray. Finally you sit down and talk about how such an arrangement would differ from life when they lived with you before. Then you set up some standards based on those new understandings.

As I thought about this new phenomenon, I was reminded of another adult son who returned home. The story is found in Luke 15.

This adult child left home, broke his father's heart, took everything that was his, traveled to a distant country and there wasted every penny on wild living. When all his money had disappeared and every other option had evaporated, he reckoned that even his father's servants fared better than he. So he made the famous statement, "I will arise and return to my father."

This ancient story hit me right between the eyes with fresh power and relevance as I read it again in light of the new patterns in our society. Note how the father reacted when he saw his long-lost son:

> But when he was still a great way off, his father saw him and had compassion, and ran and fell on his neck and kissed him. And the son said to him, "Father, I have sinned" (Luke 15:20–21).

This son's father welcomed his boy back even before the young man had a chance to say, "I'm sorry"! I think that's the way most parents function when their kids need a helping hand. We welcome them back, regardless of the personal baggage. I hope that will be true in my life if the knock ever comes at my door.

Much more likely, however, are the visits we anticipate at Christmas, Easter, or other holidays or special events. I think it's important that we keep our children's treasures safe just for these visits.

For example, Donna and I keep a couple of rooms just like they were before our children left. In one room football trophies sit neatly on shelves, surrounded by football and basketball pictures plastered over the walls. The other room looks as if it belongs to a precious little girl, with cute stuffed animals lying all over the place.

When our kids come home for a visit, we want them to feel they're really home, not staying in some faceless hotel. We don't treat these rooms as holy shrines or as untouchable memorials stuck in a time-warp of parental nostalgia, but we do want our kids to know they're still a part of our family, even though they may be living far away with families of their own.

We love it when our children visit and we covet our time with them. It's so good to be a family!

Parenting is forever

My last point may seem like a contradiction to the thrust of this chapter, but it's not. Yes, strings turn to wings—but parents never turn into something other than parents. Once a parent, always a parent. Parenting is forever.

Some years ago I was preaching in New York about how parenting really is forever. A man stood up in an open question-and-answer time and said, "You know what you said, Pastor, about once being a parent always being a parent?"

"Yes," I replied.

"Well, it's really true! I have this friend. His kids are married and grown and all he does is worry about them, all of the time. Do they eat right? Do they dress right? Are they taking care of themselves? And you know what? My friend is ninety and his kids are seventy!"

Even when strings turn to wings, our relationship as parent-to-children remains intact. We never stop being Mom and Dad, and they never stop being Son or Daughter. Author Stephen A. Bly reminds us of this fact in the following story:

> Most of the world watched the 1992 Summer Olympic Games in Barcelona. Many of us caught the action of the men's 400-meter race. For a few moments, we forgot who won, and all of us watched, instead, a British runner named Derek Redmond.
>
> He was the one who violently pulled a hamstring muscle and collapsed to the track midway through the race. With the crush of disappointment and the piercing agony of pain written on his face, he struggled to get to his feet. Olympic officials hurried to help him off the track. But with tears rolling down his face, he shoved them aside.
>
> Suddenly all of us watching at home, and most of the people in the crowd, could see what he was doing. He was going to finish the race! Years of training, hard work, and sacrifice had disintegrated on that hot Barcelona afternoon, but he was resolved to finish the race.

The pain was so great he stumbled, hopped, and hobbled. It looked for a while that there was no physical way he could go on. The race was long over when the crowd began to cheer for Derek. Even with their encouragement, it appeared that he just couldn't do it. Terrifying pain was overcoming the will to go on.

Then an older man illegally broke through the ranks of people around the track. The man walked right up to Derek Redmond and grabbed him around the chest. Derek threw his arm over the man's shoulder.

That was no official trying to get Derek off the track. That man was trying to help a courageous, determined athlete complete the race.

The man was Derek Redmond's father.[8]

I want to be a father like that!

I hope that no matter what trouble any of my children might fall into, they'll always know that standing in the crowd somewhere, ready to break through the tape, put his arm around them and help them through, is a father who loves them. A father who will love them as he's been loved by his Father in heaven.

Our Heavenly Father loves us unconditionally. He's the God of a hundred million chances who always is there to encourage and strengthen us. I'd like to believe that will be the goal for all of us when strings turn to wings.

Handing off the baton

Joseph Bayly is one of my favorite writers. For many years he edited *Eternity* magazine, wrote numerous articles, and published many books about the family. Bayly went to be with the Lord many years ago, but just before his sixtieth birthday he wrote a column for *Family Life Today* magazine in which he reflected upon his own family experience:

Sometimes God speaks to us or causes us to take a long look at ourselves and our families at a time of change. That time may be the beginning of a new year, or it may be an unexpected jolt, a coming up short. My sixtieth birthday was such an occasion, when I had a warning of my mortality, that a day is coming when my voice in this world will be stilled and I shall awaken in my Lord's awesome, joyous presence. The warning was a tap on the shoulder, not hands around my neck or a shove to the ground, but it caused me to think deep thoughts and consider separations and ponder my life and my work.

One heavy thought that came to me was what final testament I would leave for my children and other Christians of their generation. That was not a new thought. In recent weeks it had been recurrent, but now there was an edge of urgency to it. I could not avoid the evidence that my generation is in the process of turning the game over to a fresh team.[9]

When I read those words, I realized that all of us will one day hand over "the game" to our children and the next generation. It's hard to pass on the baton. Any relay team will tell you that's the most dangerous moment of the race. And those last few steps before we let go of the baton and our child picks it up are some of the most difficult steps we ever take. But if we follow the principles of the Word of God, we can make it. And God can help us grow families that honor and glorify Him. Wherever our kids may fly.

1 Carol Kuykendall, *Give Them Wings* (Colorado Springs: Focus on the Family Publishing, 1994), 140–141.

2 Ibid., 99.

3 Erma Bombeck, *Motherhood—The Second Oldest Profession* (New York: Dell, 1983), 30.

4 Kuykendall, 143.

5 James Dobson, *Focus on the Family Newsletter,* July 1989.

6 Stephen A. Bly, *Just Because They've Left Doesn't Mean They're Gone* (Colorado Springs: Focus on the Family Publishing, 1993), 21–22.

7 Ibid., 21.

8 Ibid., 180–181.

9 Joseph Bayly, "Don't Stop Loving Your Children," *Family Life Today,* July/August, 1986, 9.

Ten

It Really Is Worth It!

———

"Arise, my darling, my beautiful one, and come with me.

See! The winter is past; the rains are over and gone.

Flowers appear on the earth;

the season of singing has come,

the cooing of doves is heard in our land.

The fig tree forms its early fruit;

the blossoming vines spread their fragrance.

Arise, come, my darling; my beautiful one,

come with me."

—SONG OF SOLOMON 2:10-13 (NIV)

———

*t*he great Reformer Martin Luther is not remembered for his expertise in marriage counseling, but in a flash of insight he once gave some of the all-time best advice on building a strong home. He said, "Let the wife make the husband glad to come home, and let him make her sorry to see him leave."

At the end of the day–or at the end of a life together–it really all boils down to that, doesn't it? Strong marriages are the basis for and the *sine qua non* of healthy families. Despite whatever hardships we might face, regardless of the tragedies that might goose-step into our lives, our top priority as parents must always be to keep our marriages rock-solid.

This is a message we cannot hear too often.

That's why I wanted to end this book by saying it again.

Whatever the cost, whatever the effort required, godly marriages and the healthy families they produce are *worth it all.*

Marriage: A team event

When a person really wants to do things right, it never hurts to go back to the beginning and read the instructions. If we truly desire to build strong homes and enjoy each other deeply as husband and wife, perhaps we ought to remind ourselves why marriage exists in the first place.

> And the LORD God said, "It is not good that man should be alone; I will make him a helper comparable to him." Out of the ground the LORD God formed every beast of the field and every bird of the air, and brought them to Adam to see what he would call them. And whatever Adam called each living creature, that was its name. So Adam gave names to all cattle, to the birds of the air, and to every beast of the field. But for Adam there was not found a helper comparable to him. And the LORD God caused a deep sleep to fall on Adam, and he slept; and He took one of his ribs, and closed up the flesh in its place. Then the rib which the LORD God had

taken from man He made into a woman, and He brought her to the man. And Adam said: "This is now bone of my bones and flesh of my flesh; she shall be called Woman, because she was taken out of Man." Therefore a man shall leave his father and mother and be joined to his wife, and they shall become one flesh (Genesis 2:18-24).

> *"Christian marital love is (or should be) as close as we are likely to experience to being 'a piece of Heaven on earth,' for it is a true leftover from Paradise."*
>
> **—Mike Mason**

Marriage exists because God saw that it was "not good" for Adam to be alone. Every other creature in Eden had its mate; every other male already had paired up with his female counterpart. Adam was the only one in all of Paradise not on a team-and God said, "That's not good." And so He created Eve.

From the very beginning, God meant marriage to be a team event. From the moment the Lord brought Eve to Adam's side, the man and the woman were to function as a unit, a pair, a team. Adam was no longer a bachelor. From now on, he would eat, sleep, worship, explore the garden, and enjoy the world together with his spouse. *Together.*

Whatever life might present, Adam and Eve would face it *together.*

This part of marriage has never changed and never will change as long as wedding bells peal. As one writer has said:

> Husband and wife share enjoyable experiences and frightening ones; they share drudgery and ecstasy. A child is given to them; they stand in amazement by its cradle, and later when it takes its first step from its mother's to its father's arms. Then again they bend over it together when it is ill; it pants for breath, and the same terror grips them, and their joint prayer rises to God. If one of them is ill, the other does the work of both. If unemployment comes, they learn to economize and discover ways of dealing with the situation together.

Husband and wife share not only the past, but the future too-their joint plans and hopes and anxieties, and the joint uncertainty of not knowing at morning whether they will be together again at evening. God holds them together in his hand. Such is marriage.... This love-this bond-is used again and again in the Bible and is the only simile adequate to express God's love of man and his covenant with his people.[1]

For those who have joined their souls before God in holy matrimony, *together* is the only way to face life. And what delights are offered to those who choose such togetherness! As Norman Vincent Peale noted two decades ago, "There is nothing else like the closeness, the mutual support, the deep affection and companionship that grow between a man and a woman who have fought the battles of life together for years and years. Pleasures are brighter because you share them. Problems are lighter because you face them together. There's no describing these things, really; you have to experience them to know them. And the only way to experience them is to set one shining goal in marriage, *permanence*, and stick to it no matter what adversities you may encounter along the way."[2]

It only makes sense that, if you're chosen to be part of a team, you work hard with your teammates to win. Life is so much easier and more enjoyable that way! Is it any wonder that the Book of Ecclesiastes declares:

Two are better than one, because they have a good reward for their labor. For if they fall, one will lift up his companion. But woe to him who is alone when he falls, for he has no one to help him up. Again, if two lie down together, they will keep warm; but how can one be warm alone? Though one may be overpowered by another, two can withstand him. And a threefold cord is not quickly broken (Ecclesiastes 4:9-12).

When we choose to be married, we choose to be part of a team, the oldest and most basic team in human history. And like any team, marriage has its ups and downs. No marriage is an unblemished mirror of Paradise; all our mirrors betray cracks of one size or another and only imperfectly reflect what God intended when He brought the first woman to the first man.

Author Carole Mayhall has rightly observed, "Marriage is an enormous enigma, a colossal conundrum. It is agonizing adjusting, pain and pleasure, delight and demands. It is a mixture of the mundane, the ecstatic, the commonplace, the romantic. It comes in waves, ripples, bubbles, and splashes. Its days contain thunder, sunlight, hail, wind, rain. Its hues are the rainbow's spectrum, but prominent are shades of red, purple, yellow, and gray. It is intimacy, distance, closeness, separateness. It is a quiet melody, an earthy novel, an obscure mystery, the greatest show on earth. It is choices. Choosing to love, to understand, to enjoy, to know. It is choosing...marriage."[3]

Yes, marriage is a choice. A choice to be part of a team, a unique pairing through which God longs to display His love and goodness and glory to a needy world. Starting with the people under our roof.

Marriage: The mystery of "one flesh"

When Jesus considered the team event of marriage, He emphasized not only the cooperation and mutual benefits of husband-and-wife pairings, but more especially the mysterious union which explodes into being when a man and woman say "I do." In His own words:

> Have you not read that He who made them at the beginning "made them male and female," and said, "For this reason a man shall leave his father and mother and be joined to his wife, and the two shall become one flesh"? So then, they are no longer two but one flesh. Therefore what God has joined together, let not man separate (Matthew 19:4-6).

According to Jesus, marriage is a total commitment and a total sharing of the total person with one other, for the rest of their lives. God intends marriage to be more than two people sharing the same name; more than two people sharing the same home; or even more than two people sharing the same bed. God presents marriage as a profound biological and spiritual union which reaches to the very depths of what it means to be human.

In marriage, two people become one. Five times in the Bible God uses the term "one flesh," always to refer to that special union between a man and a woman which we call marriage. We often think that "one flesh" refers merely to the physical relationship of marriage.

It doesn't.

The "one flesh" of marriage *is* physical, but it's more than that. The term describes the full-dimensional return of a woman to the man and the completion of the man in the woman. It is physical, emotional, and spiritual. The "one flesh" of marriage is accomplished when together, a couple loves their way to wholeness by progressively tearing down the barriers of sin that grow up between them.

For the Christian couple, marriage is one new life, existing in two persons. God intends for two people–body, soul, and spirit–to be united in all three of those dimensions. The married couple doesn't morph into a single person, but the two persons in a marriage do progressively act as a single unit.

As John Piper has said:

> By creating a person *like* Adam yet very *unlike* Adam, God provided the possibility of a profound unity that otherwise would have been impossible. There is a different kind of unity enjoyed by the joining of diverse counterparts than is enjoyed by joining two things just alike. When we all sing the same melody line it is called unison, which means "one sound." But when we unite diverse lines of soprano and alto and tenor and bass, we call it harmony; and everyone who has an ear to hear knows that something deeper in us is touched by great harmony than by mere unison. So God made a woman and not another man.[4]

Although in marriage a man and woman become "one flesh," they do not cease to be individuals graced by God with differing talents and unique roles. Yet this does not make one mate superior to the other, nor does it make one partner more important to the union than the other!

Listen once more to Piper:

> When a man and woman perform a ballet and the man takes the lead and gives the cues, it never enters anyone's mind that by virtue of this he is a better dancer. On the contrary, her talent is magnified in the poised responsiveness and perfect adaptation that create a moment of art so harmonious that no one thinks about who is leading and who is following, but all simply admire the beautiful unity that the two have become. A marriage ought to be such a union—a work of art composed by the interweaving of maleness and femaleness.[5]

Who can fully comprehend what it means to be two persons, yet "one flesh"? Who among us has grasped the immensity of the mystery first proclaimed in Genesis 2:24? Thanks be to God, we do not have to master the full-orbed significance of the fact. Our blessed job is to enjoy marriage, not dissect it. I love what Mike Mason has written in his classic book, *The Mystery of Marriage*:

> After we have surveyed, as far as possible, all the other creatures in the world, eventually God presents us with one who is special, one who strikes a deeper chord in us than anyone else was able to do. Although the person may be very unlike us in many important ways, still there is something inside us which recognizes the other as being bone of our bone and flesh of our flesh, akin to us on a level far deeper than personality. This is a blood tie, an affinity of the heart in every sense. It is as if we discover an actual kinship with the one we love, which the marriage ceremony serves only to make official. To be married is to have found in a total stranger a near and long-lost relative, a true blood relative even closer to us than father or mother.[6]

That is the glorious mystery first announced in the Garden of Eden when God declared, "A man will leave his father and mother and be united to his wife, and they will become one flesh." Aren't you glad mysteries are created to be enjoyed?

Marriage: Security in love

Before sin entered the world, Adam and Eve lived perfectly secure in each other's love and needed no cover-up. Genesis 2:25 says simply, "And they were both naked, the man and his wife, and were not ashamed." Before the Fall, this first husband and wife remained selfless and free from concern about personal appearance or how much they revealed about themselves. They trusted one another and felt safe in each others' embrace.

Sin changed all that.

But despite the Fall, in Jesus Christ marriage can become open and selfless. Why? Because in Him we find a security that makes it possible to tear down the barriers and to be who we really are with the one we love. We recognize that in Jesus Christ we have nothing to prove, because in Him we are whole and complete. The security God designs for a Christian marriage keeps us from going through life with clenched fists, trying to prove ourselves to our mate.

Keith Miller got to the heart of this in his book, *The Taste of New Wine:* "The soul of marriage can be a trysting place where two people can come together quietly from the struggle of the world, and feel safe, and accepted, and loved, or it can be a battleground where two egos are locked in a life-long struggle for supremacy; a battle which in the most part, is invisible to the rest of the world."[7]

Our marriages can be either a trusting-ground or a battle-ground. The choice is ours. But how much better to live in a place where we feel secure with each other, where we're not trying to prove anything. How

"The person who sleeps next to you at night and eats across the table from you each day is eternal. Remembering that fact has a way of changing the way you treat that individual! Honoring, affirming, and cherishing become a greater desire when we know it can become part of a gift package to God in eternity."

—Tim Kimmel

delicious it feels to be married to someone who accepts us for who we are, who would never dream of asking us to prove that we're worthy of his or her love! Oh, to be secure and know that our spouse loves us not because of what we do or what we say or even how we act, but because of who we are! That's the building-block for marriage, the kind of security that will make a marriage what God intended it to be.

I agree with the wise author who said, "Marriage begins when two people make the clear, unqualified promise to be faithful, each to the other, until the end of their days. That spoken promise makes the difference. A new relationship is initiated. Marriage begins when each vows to commit herself, himself, unto the other and to no other human in this world: 'I promise you my faithfulness, until death parts us.' That vow, once spoken, once heard, permits a new, enduring trust: each one may trust the vow of the other one. And that vow forms the foundation of the relationship to be built upon it hereafter."[8]

When a husband and wife work to bring that kind of security and trust to their relationship, they can begin to enjoy the kind of marriage Carolyn Davies described in her lovely poem:

> I love you
> Not only for what you are,
> But for what I am
> When I am with you.
> I love you
> Not only for what
> You have made of yourself,
> But for what
> You are making of me.
> I love you
> For the part of me
> That you bring out;
> I love you
> For putting your hand
> Into my heaped-up heart
> And passing over
> All the foolish, weak things

That you can't help
Dimly seeing there,
and for drawing out
Into the light
All the beautiful belongings
That no one else had looked
Quite far enough to find.
I love you because you
Are helping me to make
Of the lumber of my life
Not a tavern
But a temple;
Out of the works
Of my every day
Not a reproach
But a song....⁹

Marriage: Some counsel to men

Men, do we understand the power God has given us to build loving, attractive, joyful homes? Do we understand that we have the ability, by the grace of God, to build a sanctuary out of our home, with us serving as the high priest? It's incredible, but as true as this morning's sunrise. Any husband who loves his wife gains astonishing home-building power.

But perhaps I've jumped ahead of myself. Maybe I should back up and recall from the Word of God some of its life-giving counsel to husbands who long to create households that honor God and bless others. As you read the following four passages, ask yourself three questions:

- Do I live out these passages at home?

- Does my wife see my commitment to her as expressed in these passages?

- Do my kids see a father who loves his wife in the way these passages suggest?

Now for the Scriptures:

> He who finds a wife finds a good thing,
> And obtains favor from the LORD. . . .
> Houses and riches are an inheritance from fathers,
> But a prudent wife is from the LORD
> (Proverbs 18:22; 19:14).

> Let your fountain be blessed,
> And rejoice with the wife of your youth.
> As a loving deer and a graceful doe,
> Let her breasts satisfy you at all times;
> and always be enraptured with her love
> (Proverbs 5:18-19).

> Husbands, love your wives, just as Christ also loved the church and gave Himself for her, that He might sanctify and cleanse her with the washing of water by the word, that He might present her to Himself a glorious church, not having spot or wrinkle or any such thing, but that it should be holy and without blemish. So husbands ought to love their own wives as their own bodies; he who loves his wife loves himself (Ephesians 5:25-28).

> Likewise you husbands, dwell with them with understanding, giving honor to the wife, as to the weaker vessel, and as being heirs together of the grace of life, that your prayers may not be hindered (1 Peter 3:7).

A man could spend a lifetime studying just those four texts, and not come close to plumbing their depths. But that's not the issue. We don't need to worry much about the deep end until we've mastered the shallow end. And how many of us can say we've done even that?

Several years ago when I announced at church that I was going to preach a series on the family, I received a profound letter from an anonymous woman. More than anything I could ever say, it reveals how desperately our wives need to *feel* loved and cherished.

Dear Pastor Jeremiah,

For more than a year I wanted someone to talk to as a sounding board, to share some real heart needs. But I didn't feel comfortable doing that. There is really no one to go to who won't give simple spiritual platitudes instead of practical advice, so I held everything inside.

Sometimes we Christians know that we need to go back to the basics of our Christianity to survive, but we need help, a simple nudge, sometimes a confrontive push just to get there. I'm thanking God today that He brought someone into my life a week ago who lovingly listened and lovingly confronted me without judging me. That's part of the community goal of our church, and even though my counselor was a long time in coming, I thank God for her.

The problem? I have a great marriage. What, is that a problem? When Christians have great marriages, sometimes they feel guilty and selfish when they can't deal with some little problem in the marriage. The trouble is, little foxes spoil the vines, and lately my vineyard has been pretty messed up.

All I wanted was to feel that my husband cherished me. Dating, we were exemplary Christians, but we never developed what I now see as romance. Not the kind the world brings, but a special bonding with special memories. We never had an "our song." We never sat on the beach and looked at the moon. We were involved in ministry right from the start, so, unfortunately, I never felt cherished in our relationship. I have been feeling guilty and selfish that I wanted that, to be cherished. I have been feeling selfish that I need to hear that I am loved and why. But my godly counselor helped me to see that this is entirely natural, and more important, it is part of God's plan for a Christian marriage.

As couples get older, they need to know that there is more holding them together than kids and activity, even church activity. I don't want to end up being a stranger some day to this man who I dearly love.

After my counselor listened and wisely taught me, God gave me the courage to open up to my husband in a loving, non-confrontive way, expressing my failures and asking him to help me with some of my deepest needs, even sometimes when I don't seem to know how to receive that help. We women can get very confusing to men, I know. But how I prize my dear husband for being willing to try to understand and committing to me that he won't ever give up trying. In fact, we have made a renewed commitment to be a blessing to each other, to encourage each other, to share with each other, and even to be more intimate with each other physically, emotionally and spiritually, and to begin to create special romantic moments from now on.

I just wanted you to know these things. It's the little things that make and break a marriage. Failing Christian homes are Satan's delight, but I would love for us to give God a gift-hundreds of holy, joy-filled homes from the Shadow Mountain Community Church.

Thanks for listening, Pastor.

-A "cherished" wife

It took a lot of courage for this woman to write such an honest letter. I am sure she speaks not only for many women, but for numerous men as well. As Christian people, we have all the tools we need to develop warm, loving marriages-and to help our mates *feel*, not just "know," that they are deeply cherished.

Marriage: Some counsel to women

The Bible is an equal opportunity book. God would never dream of instructing husbands about their part in creating a loving home without also giving wives some corresponding instruction. Happy and successful marriages require two active laborers. Wives, consider four scriptural gems addressed to you, while asking yourself three questions:

- Do I live out these passages at home?

- Does my husband see my commitment to him as expressed in these passages?

- Do my kids see a mother who loves her husband in the way these passages suggest?

And now for the texts:

Who can find a virtuous wife?
For her worth is far above rubies.
The heart of her husband safely trusts her;
So he will have no lack of gain.
She does him good and not evil
All the days of her life
(Proverbs 31:10–12).

Train the younger women to love their husbands and children, to be self-controlled and pure, to be busy at home, to be kind, and to be subject to their husbands, so that no one will malign the word of God (Titus 2:4–5, NIV).

Wives, submit to your own husbands, as to the Lord. For the husband is head of the wife, as also Christ is head of the church; and He is the Savior of the body. Therefore, just as the church is subject to Christ, so let the wives be to their own husbands in everything (Ephesians 5:22–24).

[Wives…] Do not let your beauty be that outward adorning of arranging of the hair, of wearing gold, or of putting on fine apparel; but let it be the hidden person of the heart, with the incorruptible ornament of a gentle and quiet spirit, which is very precious in the sight of God (1 Peter 3:3-4).

Without God's help, no woman alive could hope to live up to the lofty standards these passages set. Without the Holy Spirit at work in the heart of a godly wife, these texts would be nothing more than pipe dreams at best-and red-hot condemnations at worst. But when holy women submit themselves to the will of God and depend on the strength He promises to provide, their homes can begin to take on the aroma of godliness that wafts so sweetly from these verses in the Word of God.

> "It's in the celebration of our marriages that strength comes. It's in experiencing the joy of sharing past memories and creating new ones that strength is maintained."
>
> —Dr. Kay Kuzma

Sophia Hawthorne was one such woman, although we would never have known her name were it not listed alongside the great names of literature. When brokenhearted Nathaniel Hawthorne went home to tell his wife that he was a failure and had been fired from his job in a customs house, she surprised him with an exclamation of joy.

"'Now', she said triumphantly, 'you can write your book!'

"'Yes', replied the man, with sagging confidence, 'and what shall we live on while I am writing it?'

"To his amazement, she opened a drawer and pulled out a substantial sum of money.

"'Where on earth did you get that!' he exclaimed.

"'I've always known you were a man of genius', she told him. 'I knew someday you would write a masterpiece. So every week, out of the money you gave me for housekeeping, I saved a little bit. So here is enough to last us for one whole year.'"[10]

Sophia Hawthorne believed in her husband and encouraged him, and from her trust and confidence came one of the greatest novels of American literature, *The Scarlet Letter*.

May I tell you my personal story? Several years before *Turning Point* came into existence, we were doing a little weekend radio program called

Straight Talk with David Jeremiah. It was produced by a West Coast agency and broadcast once each weekend. We were pretty excited about it.

The program began at a time when some pretty tough things were hitting us. Donna's father had just died and it seemed as if the windmill syndrome had begun to strike us hard.

One day I drove up the coast for an appointment with our producer and, without warning, he announced, "We've given some careful observation to where you're going with this program. We don't think it has national potential, so we are going to discontinue its production. We hate to say this to you, but we have a lot of other people who need our help. So, you can do whatever you want, but we don't think you have a viable ministry in the national arena."

Stunned, I walked out to my car, got in, sat down, and wept. God had put the radio broadcast in my heart-what was I to do now? I drove home with a crushed spirit. When I walked into our home, I said to Donna, "You aren't going to believe what happened today," then laid out the whole, sad story. I never expected to hear what she said next.

"Last time I knew," she declared, "God was in charge of viable ministries."

Today, because of the encouragement of my loving wife, *Turning Point* is carried by several hundred stations.

Women, you will never know the importance of your encouragement to your husband. How desperately we need your positive words at just the right moment! You wield an awesome power that can literally change the future.

If I had to pick one other time in our family history that demonstrated what it means to *feel* love, I would drift back to a chapter in our life when we had just begun our ministry in California. We had been here for eighteen months and made some needed changes in church personnel, some of which I initiated and some of which occurred through the normal changing of the guard. Not all of these changes were perceived positively, and a few people got downright hostile. One day I came out of my office to find my secretary visibly shaken.

"What's wrong?" I asked.

"I just got a phone call from a very angry man in our congregation who told me he has been collecting names on a petition to demand your resignation," she said shakily. "He thought that by tonight he would have over a hundred names–and he plans to bring his petition to the business meeting."

To that point in my life I had never become the target of such hostility. I had enjoyed a good amount of success and had received mostly positive feedback. Those angry words were almost more than I could handle.

In the providence of God, my wife happened to be in the office that day and heard everything. Together we retreated into the quietness of my study and closed the door.

"Honey, I'm so sorry," I began. "I don't know what's going to happen tonight, but I feel so responsible for bringing you into this environment. I'm responsible for the insecurity you must feel and I feel just awful. I'm sorry that you even had to hear this." Then we cried together.

Moments later, without batting an eye, she looked me square in the face and said, "David, that's one thing you never have to worry about. The kids and I are not concerned about our future; it's a future with you. God will always have a place for you and we love and believe in you more than you will ever know. So don't worry about tonight. It's OK."

That encounter graced me with a deep and precious memory. Before that moment, everything I had hoped for in life and ministry seemed threatened. But Donna made me realize the crisis really didn't matter, for I had a wife and four children who deeply loved me. Whatever else might happen in the world outside that little room was quite unimportant.

You see, if we're loved at a level where we can *feel* it, we hold a possession money can never buy. That day my wife and family gave me a good dose of usable love...and it hasn't run out yet.

Marriage: With Christ at the center

It's no accident that in the New Testament God says the relationship of a husband to his wife is like the relationship of Christ to His church. God intends that we develop a wonderfully intimate relationship with the precious person He has given us to be our husband or wife.

Peter Marshall described the relationship God wants us to enjoy in our marriages like this: "Marriage is not a federation of two sovereign states; marriage is a union, domestic, social, spiritual and physical. It is a fusion of two hearts, the union of two lives, the coming together of two tributaries, which after being joined in marriage will flow in the same channel-in the same direction, carrying the same burdens of responsibility and obligation."[11]

Marriage is two tributaries coming together to flow in the same channel, forever. In Christ-and only in Christ-that's a possibility. As David Mains has written:

> Those who follow Christ have a much better chance at accomplishing the Bible's odd mathematics of marriage, of making two become one. Why? Because such people bring an expectation of gradual growth to their marriage. They expect time to act as their friend as they live together. Such a mindset not only carries them past unexpected setbacks, but also gives them an assurance that added years of maturing can only better their current condition.[12]

A beautiful wedding service at our church a few years ago affected me so deeply that I almost cried during the ceremony. The following piece is part of what touched me so powerfully:

> Two persons who are both related to the Lord Jesus Christ and to each other in marriage have Christ as the unifying center of their shared life. This center is outside of themselves, transcending their individual wills with His will, their strength and their love with His love. Just as they are individually united with Him, they are united with each other.
>
> The Lord God made woman out of part of man's side and closed up the place with flesh, but in marriage He reopens this empty, aching place in man and begins the process of putting woman back again, if not literally in the side, then certainly at it. Permanently there, intrusively there, a sudden life-long resident of a space that

until that point the man will have considered to be his own private territory, even his own body. But in marriage man will cleave to the woman, and the woman to him the way his own flesh cleaves to his bones. "Just so," says the Lord, "do I myself desire to invade your deepest privacy, binding you to me all your life long and even into eternity with cords of blood."

God desires that our relationship with each other in marriage reflect the intimacy we have with Him! Giving all of our energy to cultivate oneness and intimacy with each other works wonders in fending off threats to our marriage.

But how best to use that energy? What mind can best direct it? What Guide can most effectively help us work diligently to create a great marriage?

I believe with all of my heart that for marriage to become the treasure the Bible says it can be, Jesus Christ must be at the center. That's the reason Jesus Christ came into the world: to tear down the barriers between a man and his God and ultimately to tear down the walls between a man and his fellow men and women.

> *"I know of no realm of life that can provide more companionship in a lonely world or greater feelings of security and purpose in chaotic times than the close ties of a family. As tough as it may be to maintain this closeness, I say again, it is worth every ounce of effort."*
>
> **—Chuck Swindoll**

When Jesus Christ comes into a life, he or she gains the basic equipment necessary to become "one" with another person, to be a person secure in identity, someone who doesn't have to prove personal worth because he or she recognizes that worth in Jesus Christ. The best thing that can happen to any of our marriages is to come to know Jesus Christ as our personal Savior and to walk with Him by faith.

Some time ago a young couple came to see me. The woman's father is a good friend of mine who that summer had asked, "Would you talk to my daughter and her husband? They're having some problems."

I don't do much marriage counseling because of my other ministry responsibilities-besides, other counselors on our church staff do a better job than I-but I wanted to fulfill my friend's request since I met him outside our church.

As this couple and I sat down to talk, I did what I customarily do. "You know, before we go too far," I said, "I need to find out where we are. I'd like to ask you a couple of questions."

I turned to the man and asked him, "Have you come to the place in your spiritual life where you can say that you know for certain that if you were to die tonight, you would go to heaven?"

"Oh my, no," he replied.

So I began to talk about Jesus Christ and shared with him the Gospel, the simplicity of the Good News of Christ. I told him that if he would admit he was a sinner, he could receive Christ as his Savior, who had died on the cross in his place and who rose again that he might receive eternal life. After a profitable time of questions and answers, I asked, "Does this make sense to you?"

"It sure does," he said.

"Would you like to pray right now and receive Jesus Christ as your Savior?" I asked.

"I sure would," he responded.

We joined hands together in my study and with tears rolling down his face, he prayed to receive Jesus Christ as his Savior. His wife already knew Christ, and when we all got done rejoicing, I gave them both some homework. As they prepared to leave I said, "We'll have to get back together next week so we can start working on these problems."

The husband flashed me a broad grin and declared, "I think we took care of the major one today." He was right.

When Jesus Christ is not at the center of a marriage, anything that can be done to patch up its problems serves only to hold the union together until the next problem hits. But when Jesus comes to live at the center of a marriage, a truly awesome oneness becomes possible. I like to think of it as a triangle. A man related to his God; a woman related to her God; and a husband and wife wonderfully related to each other.

Would you like to know a priceless secret? Here it is: God is awesome and He'll change your life, He'll change your marriage, He'll change your family, He'll change your future for generations to come.

That's what God, through Christ, will do!

But God is waiting for you to give Him an invitation into your life. He does not barge in where He is not wanted. If you will take the initiative today, you can begin right now to live as you were meant to live. When you do, you will start to personally experience the awesomeness of God at work in your marriage and family. And when that happens, anything is possible, as Grace Noll Crowell has said so well in her poem, "So Long as We Have Homes":

So long as we have homes to which men turn at the close of day,
So long as we have homes where children are and women stay,
If love and loyalty and faith be found across these sills,
A stricken nation can recover from its gravest ills.
So long as we have homes where fires burn and there is bread,
So long as we have homes where lamps are lit and prayers are said,
Although a people falter through the dark and nations grope,
With God, Himself, back of these little homes we still have hope.[13]

1 Theodore Bovet, "This Is Love," J. Allan Peterson, ed., *For Men Only* (Wheaton, Ill.: Tyndale House Publishers, 1973), 61.

2 Norman Vincent Peale, "Worth Fighting For," *Guideposts*, February 1977, 13.

3 Jack and Carole Mayhall, *Marriage Takes More Than Love*, rev. ed. (Colorado Springs: NavPress, 1996), 246..

4 John Piper, *Desiring God, Tenth Anniversary Edition* (Sisters, Ore.: Multnomah Publishers, 1996), 179–180.

5 John Piper, wedding homily for John and Kristen Ensor, June 10, 1978.

6 Mike Mason, *The Mystery of Marriage* (Portland, Ore.: Multnomah Press,), n.p.

7 Keith Miller, *The Taste of New Wine* (Waco, Texas: Word Books, 1966), 46.

8 Walt Wangerin, *As For Me and My House* (Nashville: Thomas Nelson Publishers, 1987), 18.

9 Mary Carolyn Davis, "Love," *Best Love Poems of the American People*, Hazel Felleman, ed. (New York: Doubleday, 1936), 25–26.

10 Jack Canfield and Mark Victor Hansen, *Chicken Soup for the Soul* (Deerfield Beach, Fla.: Health Communications, Inc., 1993), 213.

11 Eugene E. Brussell, ed., *Webster's New World Dictionary of Quotable Definitions* (Englewood Cliffs, N.J.: Prentice Hall, 1988), 353.

12 David and Karen Mains, *Living, Loving, Leading* (Portland, Ore.: Multnomah Press, n.d.), 89.

13 Grace Noll Crowell, *Light of the Years* (New York: Harper & Row, 1936).

Epilogue

A Personal Word

ebster defines an epilogue as "a speech, short poem or the like, addressed to the spectators, and spoken after the play." It may also be, "a concluding section, serving to complete the plan of the work." For my purposes, I like the first definition best. The play is over, the story of the family has been told, and I get to walk back out on stage and say a few final words to the spectators . . . in this case, my readers.

As I write, it is Thanksgiving weekend and Donna and I are snuggled up in a beautiful mountain condominium in Blowing Rock, North Carolina. In our thirty-five years of marriage, this is the first Thanksgiving that I have not watched the morning football game on TV and sneaked bites of whatever's cooking in the kitchen. Thanksgiving Day normally boasts an aroma all its own, a tantalizing scent that calls me back to dozens of Thanksgivings past.

But on this Thanksgiving morning, the only aroma filling our hideaway is the smell of an English muffin I popped in the toaster for breakfast.

How did this happen? Well, our oldest daughter Jan and her husband John are celebrating the holiday with John's parents. It's their turn! David Michael, our oldest son, and his wife, Cami, are in Virginia, showing off our grandson and celebrating Thanksgiving with Cami's family. It's their turn too! Our youngest daughter Jennifer is spending the holiday with her boyfriend's family in Northern California. And we are here in North Carolina, with our youngest son Daniel . . . waiting for the first college playoff game of the football season. We just found out we will be eating Thanksgiving dinner with the entire Appalachian

State University football team in the college cafeteria.

It's quiet here today. Almost silent. The phone does not ring. The adjoining condos are mostly empty. Last night I stayed up late reading by the fireplace and still got up early this morning. I have read and reread the manuscript that you now hold in your hands as a book...and I have to tell you it has been a powerfully emotional experience for me. Life has a way of spreading out a family's intense times, but when you record those times in a book and then spend a couple of hours reliving them all, it's almost too much to handle. Especially if you're the father in the story.

It suddenly occurred to me today that families are the birthplace of strong passions. You might say families are surging emotions-about-to-happen.

I cried on June 29, 1963, the day I saw my beautiful bride Donna gliding down the aisle to my side. She was even more awesome than I had imagined she would be.

One Saturday afternoon years later I laid across the bed in our apartment and wept as she told me of the miscarriage of our long-expected first child.

A different kind of hot tears coursed down my cheeks when I held our daughter Jan in my arms for the very first time. In fact, while I was a never-go-into-the-delivery-room kind of father, I lost my emotional cool with the entrance into the world of each of our four children.

You'd think by number four, it would have become routine. But it never did.

My emotional reserve caved in again at all the commencements. Even at a couple of eighth-grade graduation ceremonies. My last educational emotional meltdown occurred this past May when I delivered the graduation address at Christian Heritage College. Jennifer was one of the graduates. I decided to present the address as if I were having a fireside chat with her.

It had seemed like such a novel, creative idea.

And then I saw her.

My great plan collapsed like a house in a California mudslide the moment I looked into that beautiful face from the dais. Seeing that radiant smile, so full of love and encouragement, I instantly wished I had chosen some more generic approach to the speech. (I listened to the tape recently and noted several long and awkward pauses, followed by some pretty shaky reentries into the address.)

Then there was the day David Michael Jeremiah and Cami Todd were united in holy matrimony at the North Main Baptist Church in Danville, Virginia. I was the father and the preacher, and maybe that wasn't such a good idea, either. Somewhere between playing those two roles, I lost sight of the ceremony I was trying to read. I tried to choke back the tears, but what started as a mist soon turned into a shower!

It happened again in the garden outside of the Lowes Hotel in Coronado as I officiated at the marriage of Jan and John. On at least two occasions I had to stop and collect my strength. I know I'm not exaggerating, because an entry in my personal journal, written the following day, records several embarrassing details of my performance.

Our grandson, David Todd Jeremiah, was born at 2:30 A.M. on August 25, 1997. Because he was premature and suffered some early problems, he was placed in the intensive care nursery. His father and I were the first to visit him there. When I saw all the tubes and wires hooked up to his tiny body, I distinctly remember turning away my head and biting my lip until it bled. What a moment that was!

Most of the time, our tears have been the overflow of joy from some wonderful event in the life of one of our kids.

But there have been the other kind of tears too.

I will never forget the day in a shopping mall in Portland, Oregon, when I learned in a telephone conversation that my mother had died. I wandered through the mall, trying to find my family. The first person I ran into was Cami. At that time she had not yet become my daughter-in-law, but she comforted me and encouraged me as if she were already a part of the family.

And how could I forget the night in a New Hampshire hotel when I had to tell Donna that I had cancer? From that time to this, we have endured innumerable ups and downs as we rejoiced over good exam reports and wept over those that were not so good. One of the hardest moments of recent days occurred when I had to tell Daniel that my disease had recurred. We spoke in the parking lot outside the Mello Mushroom restaurant in Boone, North Carolina, after his football game was over. Donna and I were about to return to San Diego...leaving him there to deal with thoughts of the sobering message I had just conveyed.

Epilogue

On one of his leadership tapes, my friend John Maxwell tells about recruiting team members for an organization. He always asks a prospective leader, "What do you cry about?" It may seem like a strange interview subject, but John is absolutely right about its importance. The things that bring us to tears tell much more about ourselves than we know. Washington Irving said, "Tears are the mark of power. They speak more eloquently than ten thousand tongues." And somewhere I read about words that weep and tears that speak.

For much of my life, I have tried to hide my tears and push them back down inside where no one would notice. But recently I have been discovering that my tears are the express lane from my soul. They are the exclamation points that punctuate my life with importance and meaning.

Yes, I cry about my family (and it seems to be getting worse rather than better). More than ever, I am thankful for our home. I am thankful that early in our marriage, we decided to make our family a priority. We have never regretted that decision. Our conviction has been tested often, but never lost from sight!

Looking back at these thirty-five years of family life, Donna and I need say no more than this: "We made it, and so can you." On your way you will enjoy many wonderful moments. Some people call them Kodak moments. For me, they always seem more like Kleenex moments!

Yes, there will be tears, my friend. Strong emotions come with the job description of mom and dad. Our Lord Jesus, no stranger to tears Himself, sees every tear shed…even the secret ones you may think no one notices. With His help, His wisdom, His priorities, His forgiveness, and His daily infusion of strength, many of those parenting tears can be tears of joy.

God is the Giver of all good gifts. Even the ones wrapped in pain.

David Jeremiah
Boone, North Carolina

TOPICAL INDEX

Topical Index

Cain, 40
Caleb, 109, 110, 115
Calvin, John, 168
Cambridge University, 91
Canaan, 109
cancer, 95, 229
    diagnosis of, 83
captives, 108
    Hebrew, 102, 106
captivity, Babylonian, 107
career, 24
Carmichael, Amy, 121, 122
Cedarville College, 187, 196
celebration, 218
center, spiritual, 83
centerpiece, God as, 64
challenge, 137
challenges, 75, 78, 137
change, power to, 223
changes, 200, 201
character, 62, 100, 110, 150
charismatic, 194
Charles I of England, 133
child abuse, 32
child-rearing, 12, 14, 15, 25, 45, 143, 195
    privilege of, 19
childbearing, 29, 40
children, 140
    as a heritage, 194
    as God's gifts, 39-42
    as living messages, 186
    godly, 165, 195
choice, marriage as, 208
choices, 110, 113, 131
    importance of, 109
Christian Heritage College, 226
Christian home, 35
Christianity, 116
Christianity Today magazine, 83
Christianity, benefits of, 81
church, attendance, 145
    as guardian of Scripture, 62
Churchill, Winston, 146
Coleridge, Samuel Taylor, 169
comfort, 163
    in grief, 227
commandments, 33, 82, 162, 182
commitment, 30, 53, 87, 94, 105, 114, 134, 213, 217
    in marriage, 208
    religious, 83
    spiritual, 169

    to Christ, 177
    to God, 103
commitments
    lasting, 146
communication, 43, 53, 74
    with children, 195-197
Communist China, 103
companionship, 207
compromise, 116
computers, 196, 197
conception, 40, 54
confession, 167
confidence, 48, 105, 126, 127, 132, 149
confirmation, secular, 71
confusion, 62
conscience, 103, 173
consistency, 105, 106
continuity, generational, 89, 90
    spiritual, 91
conundrum, marriage as, 208
conversion, 176
conviction(s), 61, 105, 107, 110, 111, 115, 136, 149
    Christian, 145
correcting, 61
corruption, 62
courage, 51, 99, 100-109, 113-116, 129, 134-137, 152, 216
courtesy, 105
covenant, God's, 207
criticism, 49, 50
Cromwell, Oliver, 133
Crowell, Grace Noll, 224
cruelty, 122
crying, 52, 53, 67, 190, 191, 220, 226, 228
culture, 44, 50, 63
culture, Babylonian, 102
    differences of, 181, 182
    modern, 163, 197, 198
    pagan, 103, 104, 177
    as toxic environment, 28
    tragedy of modern, 75
    uncertainty of, 60
curiosity, 126, 163
Curran, Dolores, 144
curses, generational, 89
Cyrus, 105, 106

Daniel, 101-116, 123
    life of, 102
Darius, 106
dating, 75

230

Topical Index

Topical Index

SCRIPTURE INDEX

Scripture Index

John 3:16, 179
John 4, 69
John 10:10, 94
John 14:14, 68
John 15:7, 68

Acts 7:22, 104
Acts 16:1, 165
Acts 16:2, 169
Acts 23:11, 102
Acts 27:22, 25, 102

Romans 4:18–22, 69
Romans 5:20, 90

1 Corinthians 3:8, 176
1 Corinthians 11:1, 144
1 Corinthians 13:7-8, 31

2 Corinthians 2:14, 93
2 Corinthians 6:16, 168
2 Corinthians 9:8, 12, 69

Ephesians 3:20, 69
Ephesians 5:22, 33
Ephesians 5:22–24, 217
Ephesians 5:25, 33
Ephesians 5:25–28, 214
Ephesians 6:1, 33
Ephesians 6:2–3, 82
Ephesians 6:7, 25
Ephesians 6:13, 111

Philippians 3:17, 144

Colossians 3:16, 168

1 Thessalonians 4:5, 177

2 Timothy 1:1, 169
2 Timothy 1:14, 168
2 Timothy 1:5, 165
2 Timothy 3:2, 33

2 Timothy 3:14–15, 168
2 Timothy 3:15, 165
2 Timothy 3:16–17, 60, 61

Titus 2:4–5, 217

Hebrews 7:25, 69
Hebrews 9:27:, 179

James 1:5, 12
James 3:17, 165
James 5:16, 69, 76

1 Peter 3:3–4, 217, 218
1 Peter 3:15–16, 171, 172
1 Peter 3:7, 214

2 Peter 1:21, 60